City of Sunderland College

Hylton Learning Workshop

This book is due for return on or before the last date shown below
Please be aware that fines are charged for overdue items
Renew online: http://heritageonline.citysun.ac.uk
Renew by phone: call 5116231

BUILD YOUR OWN RAINBOW

.

BUILD YOUR OWN RAINBOW

**A WORKBOOK
FOR CAREER AND
LIFE MANAGEMENT
by
Dr Barrie Hopson
and Mike Scally**

For a complete list of books published by Management Books 2000
visit our website on www.mb2000.com

First edition published 1984 by Lifeskills Publishing Group

Second edition published 1991 by Mercury Books, London

This new edition published 1999 by Management Books 2000 Ltd
Cowcombe House,
Cowcombe Hill,
Chalford,
Gloucestershire, GL6 8HP
Tel: 01285-760722 Fax: 01285-760708
e-mail: 106002.3004@compuserve.com

Printed and bound in Finland by WSOY

British Library Cataloguing in Publication Data is available

ISBN 1-85252-300-X

THE AUTHORS

Dr Barrie Hopson

Barrie is co-founder of Lifeskills International Ltd and is now Co-Chairman. Previously, he was Joint Managing Director of Lifeskills and then Joint Managing Director and subsequently Chairman of Hay-Lifeskills Ltd.

Prior to this, he set up the Counselling and Career Development Unit and was its first Director until 1984. He has worked widely as a consultant to industrial and educational organisations in the UK, USA and Europe. He was responsible for setting up the first career counselling service in British industry in 1970 (at ICI) and has since helped a number of organisations in different countries to set up quality service and employee development systems. He is a professional Associate of the National Training Laboratories for Applied Behavioural Science in Washington DC, a Fellow of the British Psychological Society and a Fellow of the Institute of Management.

He has written twenty-two books and numerous articles on personal and career development, quality service, transition and change management, generic training skills, marriage and lifeskills teaching.

Barrie's current consultancy activity is largely spent setting up, designing and helping to evaluate major employee and management development initiatives in companies in the UK and in Lifeskills ventures in Asia and eastern Europe.

Mike Scally

Mike is co-founder and currently Co-Chairman of Lifeskills International Ltd, a people development company which works with major businesses in the UK and abroad. He was formerly Deputy Director of the Counselling and Career Development Unit at Leeds University between 1976 and 1984, having a key role in many training programmes and national projects promoting empowerment and self-management.

Mike has led people development, culture change and service excellence programmes in major companies in the retail, financial services, communications, travel, hospitality, pharmaceuticals, manufacturing and local government sectors, and has taught widely on national and international management programmes. He has written many books and articles on themes such as teaching Lifeskills, career development and creating customer-driven organisations.

Mike also serves on the Board and management committees of, and is consultant to, a range of agencies supporting development in the Third World.

*Dedicated to our families,
friends, colleagues and associates
who have contributed so much
to shaping our lives and careers.*

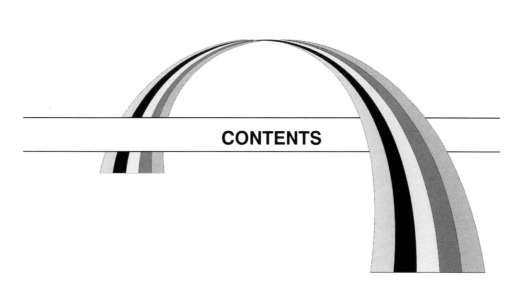

CONTENTS

INTRODUCING THIS WORKBOOK

ROUTE MAP

for the contents of this section

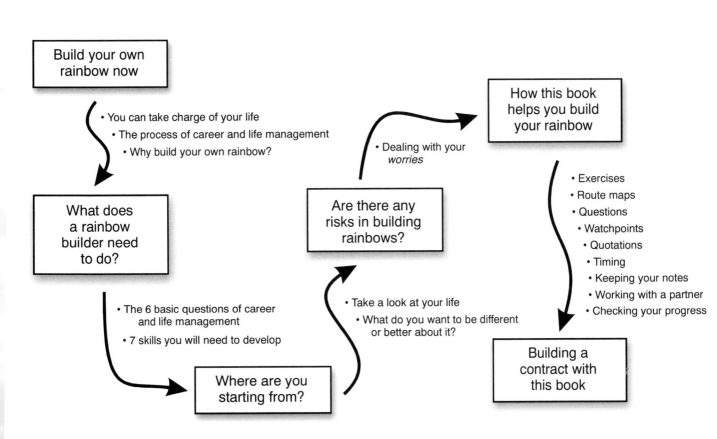

Build your own rainbow now

- You can take charge of your life
- The process of career and life management
- Why build your own rainbow?

What does a rainbow builder need to do?

- The 6 basic questions of career and life management
- 7 skills you will need to develop

Where are you starting from?

- Take a look at your life
- What do you want to be different or better about it?

Are there any risks in building rainbows?

- Dealing with your *worries*

How this book helps you build your rainbow

- Exercises
- Route maps
- Questions
- Watchpoints
- Quotations
- Timing
- Keeping your notes
- Working with a partner
- Checking your progress

Building a contract with this book

BUILD YOUR OWN RAINBOW NOW

'Here is Edward Bear, coming downstairs now, bump, bump, on the back of his head behind Christopher Robin. It is, as far as he knows, the only way of coming downstairs, but sometimes he feels there really is another way, if only he could stop bumping for a moment and think of it.'

A. A. Milne, Winnie the Pooh

Edward Bear's experience is, unfortunately, not totally unfamiliar to most of us at times. We may be aware of a vague dissatisfaction or perhaps even a major problem. We worry, we feel anxious, we do not seem to be getting anywhere. Indeed, we are not sure just where we would like to get to or even how to recognise that we have arrived. That is exactly the time to 'stop our world' and to get off; to examine our lives from the outside and ourselves from the inside.

There is a game people often play with themselves called:

'It will be different when....

- I've passed my exams
- I've left school
- I've got my promotion
- I've changed jobs
- I'm married
- We've got children
- The children leave home
- I retire ...'

Does this sound familiar to you?

If we are not careful, the months, and then the years can go by as we wait and yet never really take charge of our own lives. The habit of waiting for things to happen can develop early in life. Hence, it is early in life that we need to begin to believe and to demonstrate that:

THERE IS ALWAYS AN ALTERNATIVE

TOMORROW NEED NOT BE LIKE TODAY

THINGS DO NOT HAVE TO BE GOING BADLY BEFORE THEY CAN GET BETTER

Each of us has 168 hours to live each week. For a 30 year old with an average life expectancy of 75 years, that equals a total of 393,120 hours left to live.

With such a huge investment of time – an ever decreasing resource – it seems not unreasonable to ask ourselves:

'What return am I getting currently on the way I am spending my time?'

'What return do I want?'

'At the end of my life, what will I need to have done to be able to say to myself, 'that was the best way I could have invested those hours'?'

You can take charge of your life

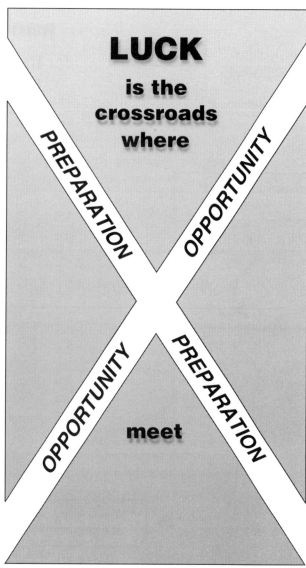

Isn't it all a question of luck?

Clearly, accidents in life happen to all of us. There will always be factors over which we have little or no control, but, in our experience, many people ascribe good or bad things that happen to them to fate, and minimise their own contributions to events.

Pinball living or self-empowerment?

Elsewhere[1] we have written about the dissatisfactions that flow from what we call 'pinball living'.

Balls in a pinball machine have no life of their own; they are set in motion by someone else and then bounce from one place to another without any clear direction, sometimes even making big scores, but then sinking into oblivion until someone sets them off again.

The opposite to pinball living is self-empowered living

Self-empowerment is a process by which we increasingly take greater charge of ourselves and our lives. To operate in a self-empowered way entails being able to:

- believe that, and operate in the belief that, we are open to and able to change;
- have the skills to change some aspects of ourselves and the world in which we live;
- use our feelings to recognise where there is a discrepancy between the way things are and the way we would like them to be;
- specify desired outcomes and the action steps required to achieve them;
- act – to implement our action plans;
- live each day being aware of our power to assess, review, influence and self-direct;
- help others to become more self-empowered.

To become more self-empowered, we need to know:

'What is important to me in life' — **MY VALUES**

'What I want to do with my life' — **MY GOALS**

'What beliefs will help me to get what I want' — **MY BELIEFS**

'What information I need about myself and our world ' — **INFORMATION**

'What skills I need to get me what I want' — **MY SKILLS**

These are the building blocks for personal change.

Why 'build your own rainbow'?

Throughout history, a rainbow has been a symbol of hope and achievement. In China, it is viewed as the bridge between this world and paradise. In India, it represents the highest attainable yogic state. In our everyday Western world, it is often viewed as ephemeral and beautiful – beautiful perhaps partly because of its ephemerality.

What do you think of when you think about rainbows?

Sit back, close your eyes. Picture a rainbow.

> What do you see?
> What feelings does it trigger for you?

We have chosen to build this book around a rainbow because to many people it represents hope, beauty, and optimism. Career and life management is a process that can enable each of us to make our lives more like we want them to be.

We depart, however, from the traditional symbol in believing that we do not have to wait for the elements to meet by chance to provide us with our personal rainbows. We can build our own rainbows. They are within the grasp of each of us.

Another part of rainbow mythology is the famed pot of gold which can be found where the rainbow touches the earth. People who try to find the elusive pot of gold by chasing rainbows are often called day-dreamers or idealists with their heads in the clouds due to their habit of hoping for impossible things. And we would agree – to a point.

There is little to gain from hoping for impossible things, but planning is the best way we know of converting the impossible into the realm of the possible.

Perhaps the 'rainbow-chasers' make their mistakes in assuming that the pots of gold are 'out there' somewhere, waiting to be found.

The true 'rainbow-builders' know that the treasure lies within themselves, waiting to be moulded and formed into images constrained largely only by the limits of their own imaginations.

The RAINBOW is the *vision*. The tools we need to build our rainbows are our *skills*. The clouds on the horizon are necessary *questions* we need to answer before we can build our rainbows.

Be a Rainbow-Builder Not a Rainbow Chaser

For a number of years, we and our colleagues at Lifeskills have been helping thousands of adults to 'build their own rainbows' in workshops in the UK, USA, Sweden, Holland, Austria and Ireland. These workshops, typically, have been for employees within organisations which have asked us to help them introduce the concept of self-managed careers into their organisational cultures. We have run them for senior management, middle management, supervisory and operative levels; for industry, commerce, the health services, social services, universities and for some Local Education Authority staffs. We have run workshops for married couples, religious groups, for secondary school staff and for youth services. We give you this roll-call not to impress you with the amount of work done but to underline how widely these techniques can be used. The principles were also published as a teaching programme for young people aged 14-19 years[2].

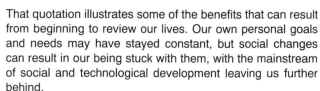

What Does A Rainbow Builder Need To Do?

The six clouds represent the six basic questions of career and life management. These are in logical sequence:

1. Who am I?

- What are my transferable skills, my values, my interests?
- How do I spend my time?
- Where do I want to live and work?

2. Where am I now?

- Which stage of life am I at?
- What kind of career pattern do I want?

3. How satisfied am I?

This will involve an analysis of all my important life roles: child, student, employee, friend, consumer, citizen, leisure-user, homemaker, and, where appropriate – spouse and parent.

4. What changes do I want?

A perfectly legitimate answer can be 'none'. This does not render the earlier questions useless. What can happen through reviewing our lives is that we may discover that we

really like much of what they contain. Reviewing our lives can provide new or renewed commitment to aspects of our present living. Many people on our adult workshops have returned revitalised to jobs, families, and lifestyle. They have discovered that they require to make some minor changes to their lives but that the major elements are fulfilling.

On the other hand, we have also witnessed some very dramatic changes. Adults have made decisions to change jobs, shift careers, get married or divorced, start a family, take up new interests, relinquish old ones. Some people discover that goals they had set for themselves years ago are no longer appropriate:

'I always thought that unless I became at least a production manager that I wouldn't have been successful, but that was what success meant to me in my twenties. It looks very different now I'm 43, so why am I still striving to get something that now I'm not sure I really want, and the striving is stopping me from enjoying what I've got.'

Workshop participant

That quotation illustrates some of the benefits that can result from beginning to review our lives. Our own personal goals and needs may have stayed constant, but social changes can result in our being stuck with them, with the mainstream of social and technological development leaving us further behind.

'What happens when people invest a good part of their lives in a contract that society rewrites?'

Gail Sheehy[3]

We may have to review not only our goals and behaviour, but beliefs that are fundamental to us but which now label us as a product of a former age.

We will also have to let our imaginations soar. There is a time for keeping one's feet on the ground but that only comes after we have soared to the limits of our imaginations. In rainbow-building we consciously encourage people to day-dream, to fantasise, to explore their ideals, to free themselves from the shackles of everyday life and its commitments.

'Your visions of the future are your assessments of the past.'

Howard Figler[4]

5. How do I make them happen?

Deciding what we want to change is the first vital step towards change. But, we all know that the road to hell is paved with good intentions. It is rarely paved with good objectives, because a good objective will lead us towards what we want to happen. The next step is to construct an action plan capable of achieving that objective. The final step is simply 'to do it' . That last step sounds the simplest but is sometimes the most difficult. It will be easier the better we become at objective setting and action planning. We may also need the help and support of other people to do this.

6. What it it doesn't work out?

However thorough our self-analysis, however brilliant our visions, however systematic our objectives and action plans, there is no guarantee that we can always build our rainbows as we want them, when we want them.

How do we cope with the frustration and disappointment when things do not turn out as we wish them to?

This is where the 'looking after yourself' skills are particularly crucial. A failed objective is simply that – a failed objective. It doesn't make you a failure. It simply means that your objective was unrealistic or not sufficiently well thought out. Failures need to be viewed more like undesirable computer feedback on a space-flight. It will be necessary to adjust course, or even abort the mission, but the promise of success will always have justified the attempt, and much will have been learned for future missions.

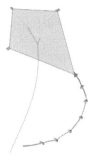

Generally it is our failures that civilise us. Triumph confirms our habits.
Clive James[5]

Skills You Will Need To Develop

Knowing yourself
Learning from experience
Research skills
Setting objectives & making action plans
Making decisions
Looking after yourself
Communicating

A rainbow builder needs to apply all seven skills listed above.

This book will enable you to develop all of these skills. You will need to be looking after yourself throughout the process. You will frequently need to communicate with others, reassess your values and skills (knowing yourself), review what has happened (learning from experience), redefine your objectives, and consequently will need to find out more information (research skills) as a result of which new decisions will need to be made. We are offering you a process, based on the **six career life management questions**.

It you follow it, it will help you to find your own answers to what you want to do with your career and your life.

Let us examine the seven skills in more detail

1. Knowing Yourself

To be a Rainbow-builder you need to have a thorough understanding of your raw materials, which in this case means you.

The analogy with building is not strictly accurate. Once objects are built, their constitution and appearance stay primarily the same. You, however, are subject to change. Indeed, the very process of introspection and analysis will influence the person you are and will become.

For effective career and life management to take place, you need information on:

- *YOUR VALUES:* what is important to you in life?

- *YOUR TRANSFERABLE SKILLS:* what you can do and enjoy doing?

- *YOUR INTERESTS:* what activities are of interest to you irrespective of your skill levels?

However, you live within the context of the life you have built, which has developed around you. Therefore, you need to know how to get information on your present style of living:

- *HOW YOU PRESENTLY SPEND YOUR TIME:* what do you do, with whom, how often, for how long?

- *WHERE YOU LIVE*

- *AT WHICH LIFE STAGE YOU ARE:* do you know what life stages there are, and where you are in relation to them?

- *WHAT KIND OF CAREER PATTERN YOU WANT:* do you want one or a number of occupations? How many hours do you want to spend in paid work? How much variety do you need?

2. Learning from Experience

Some people never seem to learn from experience. They frequently seem to repeat mistakes. Why is that? We would argue that it stems from a failure to analyse an experience to see what can be learned from it. We call this process reviewing. It involves being able to:

- *DESCRIBE AN EXPERIENCE ONE HAS HAD*
- *IDENTIFY WHAT HAS BEEN LEARNED FROM IT*
- *GENERALISE THAT LEARNING TO OTHER SITUATIONS*

3. Research Skills

To obtain self-knowledge, you need to develop the skills of looking inward, but the skills of accessing information outside of yourself are what we call research skills. You will need to know how to get information from:

- *KEY PEOPLE IN YOUR LIFE IN TERMS OF HOW THEY THINK YOU ARE DOING*
- *OTHER PEOPLE, PRINTED MATERIALS AND COMMUNITY RESOURCES*

4. Setting Objectives, Making Action Plans

A popular poster states:

'IF YOU DON'T KNOW WHERE YOU ARE GOING, YOU'LL PROBABLY END UP SOMEWHERE ELSE'

David Campbell[6]

Many people fail to get what they want in life because they have never worked out exactly what they do want. They experience dissatisfaction – they know something isn't right but they have never really developed the skill of converting complaints into aims, aims into objectives and objectives into action plans.

An **aim** is a general statement of what one wants to happen, eg, 'I want a job.'

An **objective** is an aim made more specific, eg, 'I want to get a job as a motor engineer.'

An **action plan** describes the steps that have to be completed to bring that about.

Often prior to setting objectives, we may need to let our imaginations soar to explore a wide range of possibilities.

Then we need to narrow down the possibilities.

The illustration below shows how this process occurs: first, broaden the horizons and then narrow them down.

Some people do not find it easy to let their imaginations soar and need help to learn to do so.

Objective and action planning skills, therefore, involve knowing how to:

- *CONVERT YOUR COMPLAINTS INTO OBJECTIVES YOU WANT TO ACHIEVE*
- *FANTASISE FREELY*
- *DISCOVER THE PARTS OF YOUR LIFE YOU WISH TO CHANGE*
- *SET OBJECTIVES*
- *MAKE ACTION PLANS*

5. Making Decisions

The more information you collect about yourself and the world around you, the easier it is to become paralysed by it.

The ability to generate alternative choices based upon the information, and having strategies for deciding between them is crucial.

6. Looking after Yourself

No-one has said that building rainbows is easy. Career and life management can be a demanding process.

Finding out about oneself can be very testing, intellectually and emotionally. We can unearth aspects of ourselves that make us feel uncomfortable. We may be forced to face up to very 'crunchy' and challenging questions about how we are currently living our lives. At the end of the process, with our 'Rainbows' carefully planned out, we might not be able to achieve our objectives. A vital skill, therefore, is to be able to look after oneself physically, rationally and emotionally during the process and especially when things do not turn out as we had planned.

This involves being skilled in:

- *STRESS MANAGEMENT*, and
- *STRESS PREVENTION*

7. Communicating

Career and life management will always involve a considerable degree of working by oneself. The effective use of other people, however, will be crucial to the process. We need feedback from others. We have to ask for help and information. We have to be capable of expressing ourselves clearly, orally and on paper.

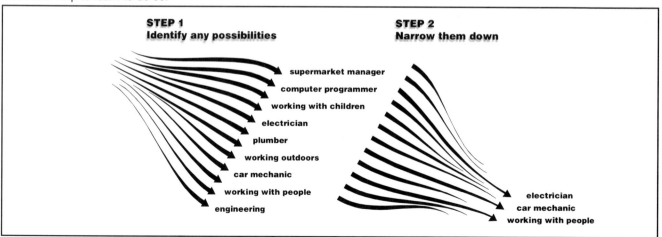

STEP 1
Identify any possibilities

STEP 2
Narrow them down

supermarket manager
computer programmer
working with children
electrician
plumber
working outdoors
car mechanic
working with people
engineering

electrician
car mechanic
working with people

Where Are You Starting From?

Your rainbow can be approached from one or many starting points. This book offers a pathway to finding and building your rainbow. All the starting points begin from a sense that 'something might be different or better' in your life.

This can range in intensity from a feeling of major crisis to simply an interest in checking out whether one is getting as much as one could out of life.

The following clouds all represent reasons commonly expressed by people for coming to our career and life management workshops.

These could also be reasons for using this book.

I find it difficult to choose among the things that are important to me.

I don't know what I want.

I want to return to a job after bringing up my children.

I want to be clearer about where I go from here in my career.

I am about to lose my job.

I'm bored, apathetic, in a rut.

I'd like to learn to accept what I've got, to feel more at peace with myself.

I'm retiring soon and I don't know what to do.

I'm quite satisfied with my job at the moment, but I feel I may be missing out on something.

I know what I want, but I don't know how to get it

I want to find out what's really important to me.

I'd like to know what jobs I'm capable of doing.

List any others that might be true for you.

Write into the three clouds below your three most important reasons for using this book.

At the end of the book, you will be reminded of these and you will be asked whether this workbook has helped you.

Take a look at your life

Lives, however hard we might try, cannot be completely compartmentalised. A job change is bound to affect other areas of your life. Changing a leisure habit may have consequences for how you spend your spare time and have an impact on your family life.

This book is designed to enable you to review your life as you are living it now, in total.

Let us examine some of the parts that together make up the whole that is YOUR LIFE.

The hardest battle is to be nobody but yourself in a world which is doing its best, night and day, to make you everybody else.

e.e. cummings

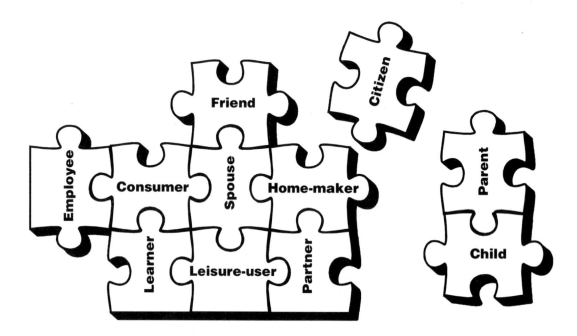

In the course of your lifetime you will occupy a variety of roles, like those in the jigsaw pieces. Sometimes they will connect with one another, at other times they will not and some will be in conflict periodically.

How you live out your life roles will be influenced by a number of other key concepts which we will examine briefly.

Work

By this we do not mean simply 'paid employment'. Work refers to activities that can provide us with:

• a sense of purpose and direction

• a structure for living, be it regular or irregular

• a personal sense of identity and self-respect

• companions and friends

• a view of how others see and feel about us.

In addition, work can provide us with money if someone wants to buy what we can do. It does not automatically provide us with money. Only paid work does that, which is why we distinguish between work and jobs. (see page 29)

We will work in the process of planning and implementing any of our life roles. We may be paid for some of that work.

Job

This is a particular position of employment one holds at any one time.

Play

This refers to activities enjoyed just for their own sake.

Income

That which is received from paid work, investments, or government benefits.

Career

This is the pattern of jobs that you have had, have or hope to have. Everyone has a 'career' in this sense, even when it is punctuated by periods out of paid employment, by retraining or learning, or whether a job varies from 40 hours a week to 1 hour a week.

Leisure

The time at your discretion – after any paid work or day-to-day maintenance activities have been done – is leisure time. It can include both unpaid work and play.

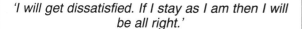
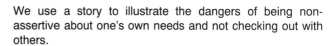

Are There Any Risks In Building Rainbows?

> *'I will get dissatisfied. If I stay as I am then I will be all right.'*

No-one should be made to review their lives. Rainbows cannot be inflicted – they have to be sought!

Our experience with adults suggests that most people benefit from occasional reviews. The parallel is visiting a GP. Many of us consult our GPs only when we are ill. We would be better advised to have periodic check-ups. As a consequence we might get ill less often.

There is no doubt that coming face-to-face with the full reality of one's dissatisfactions can be a very unsettling and sometimes painful experience. As with our bodies, however, we can only feel pain if something is wrong and needs attention. Pain is often a prerequisite to healing and growth.

'Frustration is the mother of risk'
Gail Sheehy[3]

We will sometimes have to experience the frustration before we can be motivated to want to change.

We may be happy with things as they are, but our situation may change dramatically and automatically create a problem for us. Social and technological developments may not allow us to stand still.

Remember, that you usually need storms to bring rainbows!

> *'I might want to make dramatic changes and that could create problems for others.'*

We have found all too often that people can use the anticipated fears and objections of others to mask their own anxieties and concerns. Many times we have heard statements like: 'I could never do that of course, my partner/family would never go along with it.'

Our first reaction to this concern, therefore, would be to check it out to see if it was a real concern, or whose concern it really was.

We use a story to illustrate the dangers of being non-assertive about one's own needs and not checking out with others.

For one of us (and we are not saying which one!), our in-laws arrived to spend the weekend.

My wife and I were not quite sure what to do with them, yet we felt that we should make an effort to do something. We normally looked to our weekends for recuperation and our idea of a good time is to do nothing – lie in bed and get up naturally, do exactly what we feel like doing, rarely to go out, and enjoy being at home – a luxury for us.

However, though neither of us wanted to do anything, we thought we should offer to take them out – at least on the Sunday. We asked them if they wished to go touring the Yorkshire Dales. They said they would, so we all set off. I was doing my best to be cheery, wishing all the time that I was at home reading the Sunday papers. My wife was doing her best trying to keep me happy and give her parents a good time, consequently succeeding only in giving herself a headache.

We took them to a favourite pub for lunch – which didn't do lunch on Sundays! We drove them around the Dales in a force-eight gale punctuated by occasional thunderstorms. The final straw was a puncture that I had to repair in the rain.

Six hours later when we got home, I could contain myself no longer.

'Well, I think in the future we'll stick to our usual Sunday routine!'

'What's that?' they asked. So I told them.

'That sounds wonderful. We're exhausted after the week we've had. We would have loved a quiet time with our feet up.'

'Why didn't you say anything?' I said through tight lips.

'You both seemed so determined to go out we didn't like to disappoint you. We thought that this was probably how you both liked to spend your Sundays!'

How often we make assumptions about the needs of others and remain non-assertive about our own.

But what if our desires really do clash with those people close to us?

Our answer to that would be that probably all that this process has done has brought forward in time something that would have happened in any case. Where differences exist, it is usually better to bring them out into the open where they can be examined and negotiations take place – with bargaining if need be, or at least an open discussion about the differences.

> 'What does it say about me if I keep changing my mind about what I want?'

It says, simply, that you are normal. You are more rather than less likely to change with the years .

Between young adulthood and middle-age (a 20 year period), people have been shown to change 52% of their interests, 55% of their vocational interests, 69% of their self-rated personality characteristics and 92% of their answers to questions about their attitudes. The research which demonstrated this was carried out by Kelly[7] in 1955. What would the equivalent research show today with the more dramatic rate of social change?

All too often we decide on goals for ourselves in our teens or twenties, and then we age and develop, yet still work towards goals that may not be appropriate to the different people that we have become.

'All my life – or at least it seemed that way – I had wanted to be the managing director of _____. It is only now that I realise that the real reason I wanted that in my twenties was that then I couldn't think of any other criteria of real success. It's taken me until now to realise that I have been successful in so many ways – in my work, with the family life I have created, in my circle of friends. And you know, if I really look at the way the MD lives, I wouldn't want that lifestyle. Yet, I've struggled for years to get somewhere I now know I don't want to get to and I've been giving myself a bad time for not getting there!'
(A Marketing Manager of a large company, aged 46)

We were also very impressed with some advertising copy we came across in the USA selling a particular make of car, and thought it was so relevant to career and life management:

'HAVING ARRIVED DOESN'T MEAN MUCH IF YOU'RE BORED GETTING THERE'

'Each path is only one of a million paths.Therefore, you must always keep in mind that a path is only a path. If you feel that you must not follow it, you need not stay with it under any circumstances. Any path is only a path. There is no affront to yourself or others in dropping it if that is what your heart tells you to do.'
Carlos Castenada

> 'I can have all the "fantasies" I like, but I am still limited by what's available and what I will be allowed to do.'

There is no denying that there are very real constraints operating on us no matter how self-empowered we are. Single-handedly we cannot change the economy, prevent political disasters, give ourselves superior talents that we do not possess, or turn back our biological time-clocks. But we find that people consistently over-estimate the factors over which they can have no influence and underestimate those that they can influence.

We used a poster on workshops which said:

'YOU CAN EITHER HAVE WHAT YOU WANT OR HAVE THE EXCUSE FOR NOT HAVING IT'

That, as a statement of fact, is somewhat dubious – but it makes the point.

Rainbows begin in the clouds and that is where we need to begin also. Life's constraints are all too obvious and can prevent us from exercising our imaginations. The view from the clouds can be very different from the limited horizons we can see from the ground. Having seen it, we may choose to return to earth in a different place.

Similarly, there is often a distinction between what we could do and what we think society tells us that we should do. Sometimes we fail to begin to build rainbows because we are the 'wrong' age, the 'wrong' sex, or lack 'qualifications'.

Age stereotyping is very real and happens all the time. On page 72, you can explore your own attitudes to ageing and discover how far you yourself contribute to 'ageism'. Much age stereotyping is reflected in social attitudes, rarely based on facts. Some, sadly, are reflected by real constraints still placed upon people concerning when they may enter a particular occupation. The demographic changes in the 1990s, with fewer young people available, are forcing employers to look again at attracting and developing older people.

Sex-role expectations undoubtedly are a very real barrier to rainbow-building. The work of the Equal Opportunities Commission and subsequent legislation have all helped to widen horizons for both sexes. Girls are now out-performing boys academically and are as assertive in career terms as young men are. Some even suggest that many young men have lost their way as roles have become blurred.

We all have a vital role in working for a future in which there are not two sets of rainbows – one with a pink hue and another with a blue one!

> 'I don 't like the idea of planning for the future. takes away all the spontaneity from life.'

Career and life management is not dedicated to forcing people to plan their lives away. It is dedicated to helping people gain more control over what happens to them. Neither of the present authors likes to plan more than 6-12 months ahead. That is our personal preference, but we have learned that about ourselves by discovering more about who we are and what we want from life.

Other people like to create 5-year, 10-year or lifelong plans. There is no right or wrong way. Those of us with short term inclinations could do well to force ourselves occasionally to look long term, and the lifelong planners need to remind themselves that any long-term plan needs periodic reviewing.

The seeming paradox of career and life management is that the more attention we give to reviewing our needs, determining our priorities, setting objectives, the more likely we are to provide ourselves with gift vouchers of time to exchange for anything we, spontaneously, might choose to do.

> 'What happens if I try to make changes and I don't get what I want? Aren't I worse off than before I started?'

We believe that the straight answer has to be 'NO'. Unless we risk change we will never gain access to new possibilities.

'Risk is the tariff for leaving the Land of Predictable Misery.'

Howard Figler

Rainbow building will rarely leave us worse off, even if it doesn't turn out as we would have wished. The process of career and life management will have involved us in learning a great deal about ourselves and also in using the seven crucial rainbow-building skills which we can re-apply at other points in our lives.

Perhaps the final rejoinder will always remain: ' If you don't try it, you'll never know just what you can build for yourself.'

Each of us will have opportunities sometimes. The better equipped we are with career and life management skills the greater the chance of being able to capitalise on those opportunities. Carlos Castenada talks of the importance of recognising our 'cubic centimetres of chance' – the skill of recognising chances when they occur and having the courage to pursue them.

'All of us, whether or not we are warriors, have a cubic centimetre of chance that pops up in front of our eyes from time to time. The difference between the average man and the warrior is that the warrior is aware of this, and one of his tasks is to be alert and deliberately waiting so that, when his cubic centimetre pops up, he has the speed, the prowess to pick it up.' Carlos Castenada

Remember, it is only the mediocre who are always at their best!

How This Book Helps You Build Your Rainbow

The Exercises

The book contains exercises designed to help you collect data to answer the six key questions for career and life management. These exercises are there to help you and should not represent an obstacle race. If any particular exercise does not seem relevant to you, don't do it.

Each exercise is also designed to help you apply one of the key seven career and life management skills. The particular skill or skills will be indicated at the beginning of an exercise. The exercises which are asterisked* are all ones we believe to be crucial to building your own rainbows. We have additional exercises that we also feel could be illuminating, but if time is short, you might skip or leave these until another time.

You may choose not to complete some of the optional exercises because they are not relevant to you or where you are now. Beware, however, that you may not feel like completing some of them because you may be wary of what reflections of yourself will be revealed to you . Ask yourself then if that is sufficient reason for not doing the work.

Some space is provided for writing in your answers.

Route Maps

Each of the six career and life management questions will be introduced by a ROUTE MAP that will be your guide to where answering the question will take you. The map will outline the exercises contained along the route and will summarise their purposes.

Keep a record

Periodically in the text you will see a picture of a box file. This will tell you when you need to make notes and keep a record.

You might well wish to keep your answers in an actual cardbox, but failing this, keep them in your 'AHA!' Folder (see page 21).

Occasionally, you will see a shaded card like this:

Data needed

This always refers you back to 'keep a record' files you will have from having completed earlier exercises. Your journey to building your own rainbow is not simply a straight line. There will be considerable cross-referencing.

You will sometimes be referred forward into the book. This will always be to some part of Question 6: 'What if it doesn't work out?' Throughout the book you will be invited to explore yourself, your past, your visions, your fears, your assumptions. Some of this can be very demanding and sometimes even painful. The information in Question 6 could be very useful long before you would naturally reach it in the book.

Here are some other features of the text for you to look out for:

Questions
This book constantly offers you questions to further the self-discovery process for you. These are always contained in this speech bubble.

Watch Point

This symbol will always warn you how to interpret something in the text. Watch for these! They are important.

Quotations

We 'fly' a number of quotations throughout the book in kites. These are intended to stimulate, summarize or simply amuse. Some will speak to you more than others.

Keeping Your Notes: Your AHA! Folder

A common finding in doing this kind of self-review is that many insights or 'AHA!' experiences can result from completing the exercises, and particularly in discussing them with a partner or group. We advise keeping a separate folder in which you put slips or sheets of paper with any insights that occur to you about yourself, your life or your career. There will be a stage towards the end of the workbook when we will ask you to empty the contents of your 'AHA!' Folder and use them as an aid to setting your objectives.

Remember, there are no right answers, only answers that are right for you.

The material is designed to cause reflection, to create awareness in you of your experience and the learning from that, of your skills, of how you want to shape things in the future. The 'answers' are not in the text, but in the thoughts created in you as you work through the material, in the realisations that they cause. Harvest your thoughts, look for your most significant insights. Record them!

Working with a Partner

A particular valuable strategy when faced with hours of isolated work is to link up with one other person, or even a small group of people. We would highly recommend this. Talking through these exercises not only can assist flagging motivation but other people's reactions to your efforts and thoughts are likely to be valuable and stimulating (and in turn, your reactions to their ideas could be really useful too).

A phrase we often quote is: 'it takes two to see one'. It can sometimes be enlightening to involve family, friends and colleagues in completing some of the assignments on you. It can also be scary! We do not recommend your choosing to work with someone who could feel threatened by what you are doing, or who might put you down or otherwise inhibit you.

Perhaps you could link up with some fellow 'rainbow builders' who also contract to work with the book themselves.

A clear contract is essential:

- when are you going to meet?

- how often and for how long?

- what work will you have to complete for each session?

- how will you operate as a pair or a group?

'Seen with new eyes, our lives can be transformed from accidents into adventures.'

Marilyn Ferguson

Checking your Progress

Throughout the book, there will be opportunities to pause, review your progress and see what is to come next At the end of each of the six cloud questions there is a summary chart which will help you to collect together all your data for that question.

Timing

We have deliberately not suggested times for the exercises We have found that people need to spend different amounts of time for the same exercises. We do suggest that you ensure that you have sufficient time to finish a 'block' on your route map. The end of a block is always signified by a PROGRESS CHECK.

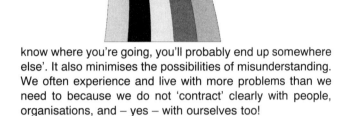

Building A Contract With This Book

By now, some goals, however hazy, might be forming in your head. Perhaps you are thinking: ' I'll give it another few pages to see if this is the kind of thing I am interested in,' or 'It really might be useful to carry out some of the exercises they are saying will follow'. We invite you, therefore, to think carefully at this stage about just what you might want from a book on career and life management. To do this we want to introduce you to the concept of 'contracting' – in itself a vital career and life management skill.

'Contracts' need not only be formal, written documents. There can be psychological contracts too, which at some stage can be written down – but not necessarily. Contracting is a process of clarifying objectives and making agreements. I can contract with a friend to go on holiday, with a partner to apportion household tasks, with a doctor to make some lifestyle changes. A contract usually involves two parties and requires us to be razor-specific about what we want, what we are prepared to do and what we expect from the other party.

The advantage of conscious contracting, as opposed to half-formed or unexpressed expectations, is that it demands clarity of objectives, and, as the poster says 'if you don't know where you're going, you'll probably end up somewhere else'. It also minimises the possibilities of misunderstanding. We often experience and live with more problems than we need to because we do not 'contract' clearly with people, organisations, and – yes – with ourselves too!

It is possible to talk of making a contract with yourself, and that is exactly what we invite you to do if you are ready to commit yourself to career and life management right now. Contracting is, for some people, really quite difficult, but we believe it is crucial. We are offering you a contract below. We have signed it. We invite you to complete this contract with us. You will be offered a chance to review it midway through the book. So, before reading any further, sit back, get comfortable, rid your mind of distractions and ask yourself the questions below.

CONTRACT
BETWEEN MYSELF AND THIS WORKBOOK

1. What will this book offer me?
This is *our* contribution to your contract. We will be inviting you to complete a number of exercises, and to answer some questions. We will be taking you on a carefully thought-out sequence of steps designed to help you ask and answer the six key questions for career and life management outlined earlier. We estimate a time commitment of approximately 48 hours to read the book and complete the assignments. This will increase if you work with a partner or a group of people.

2. What do I really want to get from reading this book? Be as specific as possible.

3. What can I personally do to make sure that I get what I want?

4. Based on past experience, what can I do to avoid sabotaging myself, thereby not getting what I want? What can I do to prevent this?

5. How do I normally feel and behave if my expectations are not being met? How helpful is this for me? What can I do to ensure my expectations will be met?

Signed by the reader

Signed on behalf of this book

Barrie Hopson   Mike Scally

Question 1
WHO AM I?

We begin with YOU as you are now. But how accurate a representation is any snapshot – an arbitrary moment of frozen time? You need to know something of your history and get a perspective on your future. YOU are the living repository of your own history, shaped by it, influenced through it and part-creator of it. To begin, focus on the context of your life to date – the events, the experiences, the peaks, the troughs, stresses sought and imposed, decisions made, decisions made for you, and the key people who populate your biography.

What you have done, been and learned so far will be your launching pad for the future.

ROUTE MAP
for "Who Am I?"

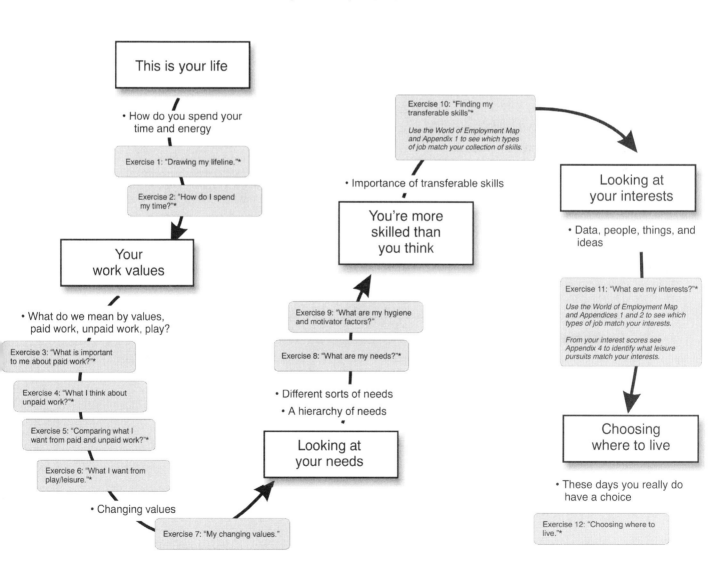

This Is Your Life

Exercise 1: Drawing My Lifeline*

RAINBOW BUILDING SKILL: Learning from experience

- Take a very large sheet of paper and draw a line which represents your life. This might be a straight line, or one with peaks and troughs – we have even seen a spiral! It's shape is to be determined by you only.

- Indicate on the line where you are NOW with a large X.

- Mark in the key events or happenings in your life on the line, starting with events as early as you can remember and proceed to the present.

- Leave plenty of space between the years. You will find that one memory triggers off another, so be prepared to move back and forth along the line as the memories flow back to you.

- Now look back at each event and ask yourself the following questions, putting the appropriate symbol or symbols after each one. For some events none of the symbols might apply.

Was this a Peak Experience – a high point, a particularly positive experience?   △

Was this a Trough Experience – a low point, a negative experience?   ∪

Was there was Important Learning for me in this?   !

How Stressful was it? Rate this on the scale:

Somewhat stressful	=	S
Stressful	=	SS
Very stressful	=	SSS

Did I take a Risk?   R

Did I Choose to do this?   √

Or did I have No choice?   X

Take as much time as you need to do this –
THIS IS YOUR LIFE!

After you have completed this, look at the following list of questions. They may not all be appropriate to you. Select those that are relevant to you or that trigger off reactions in you.

Write down your answers and add any thoughts, ideas or objectives which occur to you, and make a note of them in your AHA! Folder.

> What does this account of my life so far say about me and how I have lived my life?
>
> Does anything surprise me?
>
> What are the most important elements in my peak experiences? What have I learned from these?

This will help you to identify those things that are really crucial to you in life.

> What elements characterise the troughs or low points in my life? What have I learned from these?
>
> How much have I shaped my life and career so far - how much has been reactive?

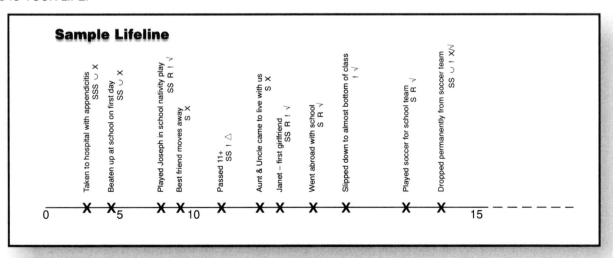

Sample Lifeline

Event	Symbols
Taken to hospital with appendicitis	SSS ∪ X
Beaten up at school on first day	SS ∪ X
Played Joseph in school nativity play	SS R ! √
Best friend moves away	S X
Passed 11+	SS ! △
Aunt & Uncle came to live with us	S X
Janet – first girlfriend	SS R ! √
Went abroad with school	S R √
Slipped down to almost bottom of class	! √
Played soccer for school team	S R √
Dropped permanently from soccer team	SS ∪ ! X√

0   X   X5   X   X10   X   X   X   X   X   X   15 – – – – –

Do I take risks? Do they turn out mostly positively or negatively for me?

Does my life divide into themes? What unfinished themes are there? Are there any changes in my life pattern with age?

What lessons do I want to apply to my next stage?

Keep a record
- My life line
- Notes about my life so far

Exercise 2: How do I spend my time?*

RAINBOW BUILDING SKILL: Knowing yourself

What you have done so far is to step back and take a long look at your life overall as you have lived it up to *now*. The next step is to examine in greater detail just how you are investing your time right now.

It consistently surprises us that we so often encounter people who spend large periods of time analysing returns and payoffs for their investments, working out the 'best buy' for a refrigerator, cassette tape or brand of marmalade, and yet do not transfer their considerable analytical skills to their own lives.

– What returns am I getting for the time and energy I am expending?

– What parts of my life are 'best buys'?

– How am I *actually* filling the hours of each day?

What we have discovered is that our memories of how we spend our time are notoriously unreliable. Weight control specialists have known for some time that asking people what they have eaten is very inaccurate. The only accurate way is to ask them to record each day what they do eat.

We invite you to do the same with your use of time.

- Over one week keep a record of your activities. Begin on any day you like, but it will be most useful if you can choose a fairly typical week and 'log it'.

- It is best done by doing the recording at the end of each day or even periodically through the day. We provide one chart below which we have found useful, but if this breakdown – into 2 hour slots – does not fit for you, do create your own. You will need a large sheet of paper.

- This is a crucial piece of data collection. You will be asked to refer back to it for Question 3, 'How satisfied am I with who and where I am?'

- This log will take you a week to complete, but you can continue with the other exercises, returning to this exercise when you have completed the log.

When your record is complete, answer the following questions:

Is this week typical of my life generally? If not, how is it untypical?

What does this 'snapshot' show me about the way I am currently spending my time?

How much of my week was spent doing things I choose to do?

	a.m.						p.m.					
TIME INVESTMENT RECORD												
	0-2	2-4	4-6	6-8	8-10	10-12	12-2	2-4	4-6	6-8	8-10	10-12
Monday												
Tuesday												
Wednesday												
Thursday												
Friday												
Saturday												
Sunday												

Fill in the bar chart below to indicate what percentage of time is spent in your different roles. (Some of your life roles will overlap so that your totals will probably be well over 100%)

TIME ANALYSIS RECORD							
Life Role	**Percentage of time spent**						
	10%	20%	30%	40%	50%	60%	70-100%
Child*							
Employee							
Spouse or partner							
Parent							
Citizen							
Consumer							
Friend							
Leisure-User							
Student/ Learner							
Home-maker							
Other							
Other							

As long as you have a parent alive you will still have a 'child' role. As our parents age and need more of our time and care that role can be very demanding.

Keep a record
- My time investment record
- Notes about the way I use time

'Each of us is potentially the difference in the world.
Marilyn Ferguson,
The Aquarian Conspiracy

'he way to succeed is to double your failure rate.
Thomas J Watson, founder of IBM

Rainbow Building Progress Check

WHO AM I?

What have you learned from reviewing your life to this point?

....

....

....

....

....

....

....

....

....

....

....

....

You have now reviewed your life overall and have examined how you spend your time right now. It is time to collect data about key aspects of yourself. The next section will provide you with information about:

Your **VALUES**

Your **INTERESTS**

Your **SKILLS**

Where you wish to **LIVE AND WORK**

What **STAGE OF LIFE** you are now at

What kind of **CAREER PATTERN** you want to have

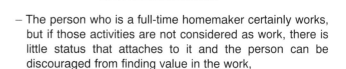

Your Work Values

Whenever you ask yourself questions like:

'Where do I want to live and work?'

'How do I like to spend my time?'

'What kind of people do I choose to have around me?'

'How important to me is money, status, autonomy, success, security, creativity, power, helping others, spontaneity, risk taking?'

you are asking questions about your values. Being able to answer questions like these, therefore, clearly plays a key role in career and life management. The more you are able to live out your values the more rewarding your lives will be.

In this section we will be focusing on what you value in WORK (paid and unpaid), and PLAY.

Work Values

On page 29, we distinguish between PAID work and UNPAID work, claiming that we will work in the process of planning and implementing any of our life roles – child, homemaker, consumer, citizen, student, employee, spouse, partner, parent, leisure-user, friend and so on.

What is Work?

- It is an activity.
- It can provide us with a sense of purpose and direction.
- It can provide a structure for living although that might be regular or irregular.
- It can provide a personal sense of identity and self-respect.
- It can provide us with companions and friends.
- It can influence how other people see and feel about us.
- It can, in addition, provide us with money if someone wants to buy what we can do.

We distinguish clearly between work and jobs. Real work is available for all of us, even if jobs are not. We must separate out the issue of income from that of work. This is not to say that income is not important. It is of crucial importance to us all, and is a political issue demanding decisions from our society on how wealth should be distributed. Everyone needs work, everyone needs income, but not everyone can get a job, in the traditional sense, nor wants one.

You may well ask:

'What is wrong with equating work with a job?'

It is not so much that it is 'wrong', but that the consequences of the link are increasingly misleading and a source of distress for many people.

– The person who is a full-time homemaker certainly works, but if those activities are not considered as work, there is little status that attaches to it and the person can be discouraged from finding value in the work,

– People who choose to be full-time parents, whilst possibly gaining a little more social status, are often still regarded and too often regard themselves as unproductive.

– People who do not have a job at all are generally thought to be unproductive and can be the focus of considerable social criticism. This is why unemployment is a social stigma still today, and why the unemployed are viewed by the employed with a mixture of concern and suspicion.

– People who choose to be employed for less than the national average, ie, for half-time or one-third time. or even four-fifths time, are sometimes viewed as lacking commitment and shirking their responsibilities.

'There is likely to be a shortage of employment as we have traditionally known it in the foreseeable future (ie, full-time jobs for life). But while there may be a shortage of such jobs, there will never be a shortage of work.'

What is taken as 'normal employment' is, of course, always historically limited to its era. Normal employment in the mid-nineteenth century was a six-day week, ten hours a day, with a week of public holidays only to look forward to.

The particular problem that we are experiencing today reflects the age old tradition of equating 'work' with 'labour', in particular, manual labour, by definition hard, often dirty and, to many, consequently demeaning. This was then linked to a peculiarly modern idea deriving from the Industrial Era. The industrial revolution demanded that vast numbers of people should leave their homes to operate machines and to service the vast bureaucracies necessary to manage the production and distribution of the new wealth. The methods of production were voracious for human labour. For many years men, women and even children were 'employed'. (The concept of employment, interestingly, cannot be found in references before 1830). It became normal for people, and increasingly just men, to have jobs in the new system, so much so, that jobs came to be synonymous with work.

In the Industrial Era the equation was born

$$WORK = JOB$$

We launched a campaign from Lifeskills Associates in the 1980s to break this equation, and we symbolized the campaign with the logo

$$WORK \neq JOB$$

Work does not equal a job. It is far broader than that.

Today, a job is typically seen as paid work involving a five-day week, seven to eight hours a day, with four weeks annual holiday. In the 21st century, this will be reduced to even shorter working weeks, up to eight weeks annual holiday and a bevy of employment alternatives incorporating job-sharing, flexitime, a compressed working week, flexiplace, industrial sabbaticals, multi-job holding, and the gradual disappearance of the concept of 'part-time' employment. It is only possible to have 'part-time' employment if there is a consensus on what 'full-time' is. Already, most new jobs created in the UK are part-time and the proportion is increasing all the time.

We can eliminate some of the confusion by looking at the different kinds of emphasis given to work throughout history These range from activities that we like doing to those that we dislike doing. Then there is work we are paid for and that for which we receive no direct financial reward. This is shown in the following chart.

TYPES OF WORK		
	LIKED	DISLIKED
PAID	A job in which the work is intrinsically rewarding. You might even do this for little or no pay.	A job involving work which you would not choose to do unless you needed the money.
UNPAID	An activity you enjoy or feel is useful. You do it for no other reason.	Activities you do not enjoy but are obliged to do by force or contractual agreement.

Types of work

We have expounded at length about the concept of WORK because we see it as being a concept central to this book, for WORK is central to each of us.

An example may help to explain why definitions of work can vary so greatly. Let us examine the activity of gardening as it might appear to different people at different times.

Liked/paid work:

This person loves gardening for its own sake. It is a source of delight to him that he actually gets paid for it also. It is his major source of income.

Disliked/paid work:

This person does not especially like gardening. If he did not have to earn money, he would not choose to do it. He does it because there are no other jobs, or because he likes this better than the other jobs available to him.

Liked/unpaid work:

This person also loves gardening but either cannot get paid for doing it or would not choose to do it as his major source of income for a variety of reasons – he likes doing other things more, or it does not pay as much as he wants to earn. This activity has traditionally been labelled a 'leisure pursuit' or a 'hobby'.

Disliked/unpaid work:

This person does not enjoy gardening. He has an arrangement with his wife, however, that he will do the gardening if she will do the housework as both agree that it needs to be done.

The scenario gets even more complicated as the nature of the work can change because the situation changes or because the person changes. For example, the disliked/unpaid work of gardening may only feel like that when you don't really have the time, the weather is disgusting or you feel unwell. Similarly, as a result of having to garden, what began as a chore can sometimes be transformed into a pleasure as you discover new facets of your skills and personality.

As an illustration of how the concepts of work and employment are changing, we reproduce for you two scenarios, one of which encapsulates the views of 40 years ago and the other demonstrates how views about work and jobs are changing so rapidly.

'We are living at at time when history is holding its breath, and the present is detaching itself from its moorings to sail across the boundless ocean'.
Arthur C Clarke

Which of the two counselling sessions that follow were closest to your experience?
(If you did not receive any vocational guidance yourself, you will almost certainly still have picked up some of the messages conveyed in these scenarios.)

Scenario: Vocational Guidance in the 1950s

In the youth employment officer's (YEO) office

YEO — 'Well, John, you're 17 now and it's time for you to choose the career in which you would like to spend the rest of your life.'

JOHN — 'What should I be looking for?'

YEO — 'That depends upon your own interests and abilities, and qualifications, but generally I would advise that you looked for a job that has good training, good promotion prospects and where you can find total satisfaction for the whole of your working life if you choose.'

JOHN — 'What if I change my mind about what I want when I've been in it for a while?'

YEO — 'Don't change your mind too often. Employers don't like it. It doesn't look good on your CV. But, if you do, you have a good education behind you, good examination results – these will keep you in good stead for any move you might wish to make in later life.'

JOHN — 'I'm thinking that a career in marketing might be for me. I enjoy travel and would be interested in a job that enabled me to travel abroad and maybe live abroad for a while.'

YEO — 'That's fine, but what will you do when you get married?'

JOHN — 'My wife would come with me. There might be an office job she could do in the company. Of course, if we had any children she will be fully occupied anyway.'

YEO — 'Quite.'

JOHN — 'What kind of holidays could I expect?'

YEO — 'Many jobs at your level now offer at least two and sometimes three weeks holiday a year. You can expect to work a basic 44 hour week, but on a salary you will be expected to work longer than that for no extra pay.'

JOHN — 'How secure is a job in marketing?'

YEO — 'It has more risks attached to it than some jobs, but the economy is booming. We are not likely to see anything like the 1930s depression again. All political parties are totally committed to full employment and there are some desperate labour shortages. You'll never be short of a job.'

JOHN — 'Of course, I do have other interests – my tennis, mountaineering, and I play the guitar. I will want to leave time for them.'

YEO — 'So you should, but be careful. Your job must come first. Your company will be investing a great deal of money in your training and will expect some loyalty and commitment in return. Do well by them and you will be well looked after for life.'

JOHN — 'Where can I learn about marketing?'

YEO — 'We have booklets which give you all the information you need on the vast range of work that's available.'

JOHN — 'Thank you. My father finds all this difficult to understand. He says I shouldn't be so choosy and just to be grateful that I've got a job.'

YEO — 'That's understandable if you think what he went through in the 30s. But today the world is your oyster.'

Scenario: Life and Career Management in the 1990s

In the career counsellor's office

COUNSELLOR   'Well, John, I know that you will have been doing a lot of thinking in your school about yourself and your future. What is important to you? How do you want to live your life?'

JOHN   'I enjoy learning very much and whatever I do I would want it to be something where I am constantly learning about new things.'

COUNSELLOR   'That will almost be inevitable whatever you decide to do. Do you know, for example, that the Electricians Union in the USA has 60 people solely rewriting textbooks because about 10% of the technical knowledge in the industry becomes obsolete each year. Also, it has been calculated that at the rate at which information is accumulating now there is four times the amount of information available than was the case when you started school. By the time you are 50 it is likely to be over 30 times greater and more than 90% of everything known will have been discovered during your lifetime!'

JOHN   'So I am always going to be learning new things?'

COUNSELLOR   'You will have to, whether it's in relation to your paid work or your unpaid work.'

JOHN   'What are my chances of finding work?'

COUNSELLOR   'Excellent! There is never a shortage of work, even if there is a shortage of full-time, permanent jobs. But in the foreseeable future, young people will be in high demand as there are fewer of you. Mind you, you may have to change your views about a job as being something you work in for 40 hours a week for 48 weeks a year for 48 years of your life.'

JOHN   'My father finds all this difficult to understand. He thinks that unless I have a job like he used to have – that I'll never amount to anything.'

COUNSELLOR   'You have to remember that life was like that when he was your age. Then you could get a job for life. Now you can expect 3 or 4 occupational changes in your lifetime, 3 or 4 job changes every 10 years. There will be some periods of your life with no job at all, and others where you will be employed but for considerably fewer hours than your father was used to. Our views about jobs and work are having to change dramatically.'

JOHN   'So you're saying that I will need to find what kinds of work I want to do, but that I will only get paid for some of it?'

COUNSELLOR   'That's right. You can find interesting work at home, in your leisure time, doing things in the community and by learning new things at college, through home study, TV courses, etc.'

JOHN   'But my father says I need a job with prospects, a job for life.'

COUNSELLOR   'You may, of course, get one, but don't bank on it. Even if you do, what he understood by a "job for life" would be very different. Then it meant until you retired at 65. As you know, the majority of large organisations now ease people out at 50 or before to begin new careers or to retire or to be partly retired.'

JOHN   'I'd like a job where I could travel and maybe live abroad, like in marketing.'

COUNSELLOR   'What would happen if you got married?'

JOHN   'Well, we would have to talk it through see whose career was most important at that time. My career might have to wait its turn. But I want my wife to have a career, because with two incomes we will both be freer to do what we want if either of us gets dissatisfied.'

COUNSELLOR   'I think you would do well to get a variety of experience. Employers are sometimes suspicious of people who never move. It looks as though they are not taking any responsibility for their own careers.'

JOHN   'But I think employers should look after their staffs.'

COUNSELLOR   'They used to – and demanded loyalty in return. They can't expect that any more. These days you need to manage your own career, and they expect that. Tell me, what else are you interested in?'

JOHN   'I enjoy programming my computer – in fact I've got quite a reputation as a debugger and chaser of 'glitches'. I play electric guitar and have started to compose some music on my computer. I play football, enjoy cooking – especially Chinese, and help my mother out on Saturdays at a market stall, selling computer games and equipment for home micros.'

COUNSELLOR   'If you're not successful in getting in to marketing, there would appear to be a number of other income-producing possibilities, plus, you certainly seem to have a full life.'

JOHN	'I'm never bored. In fact there never seems to be enough time. But how do I find out more about marketing?'
COUNSELLOR	'I'll book you some time at our computer terminal. It will help you to discover your skills, interests and identify your key values. It will then suggest a number of options. You can call up some information there and then and take a printout home with you. I can also lend you some videos to show at home on life in marketing or whatever other occupations you would like to explore. The computer will talk to you at first in terms of grouped jobs rather than specific jobs, and will relate your profile to them. You are almost certainly equipped for a far wider range of jobs or groups of jobs than you will be aware of right now.'

The next thirty years are likely to see an even more rapid rate of change which will contain its own set of unpredictables. Some of the future we can predict – the problem is that we cannot be certain of which bits. What we can be certain about is that we will all have to be more flexible and adaptable than at any other time in our history. To equip ourselves for unknown scenarios, we will need the broad range of personal competencies that we call 'Lifeskills' – knowing not just how to read and write, but how to find and use information, how to make, keep and end relationships, how to manage change, how to be assertive, how to learn, how to give and receive feedback, how to manage stress, how to make decisions and solve problems, how to manage time, how to communicate, manage conflict, develop self-confidence, and to discover what we want to do with our lives.

Paul Valery remarked that the trouble with our time is that the future is not what it used to be!

'By working faithfully 8 hours a day you may eventually get to be a boss and work 12 hours'.

Anon

RAINBOW BUILDING SKILLS: ***Knowing yourself***
Making decisions

On the four separate sheets marked 'MY VALUES CARDS' on pages 33 to 39, you will find cards to cut out which include 5 with the following headings:

VERY IMPORTANT

IMPORTANT

QUITE IMPORTANT

OF SOME IMPORTANCE

NOT IMPORTANT

- Cut out the pages indicated and then cut up the cards so that you have a pack of 35 Work Values cards and 5 heading cards.

- Place the 5 heading cards in front of you as indicated:

VERY IMPORTANT	IMPORTANT	QUITE IMPORTANT	OF SOME IMPORTANCE	NOT IMPORTANT

Look at each of the 35 work values cards and ask yourself the question:

'How important is this aspect of work to me when I am considering PAID WORK?'

- After sorting the cards into 5 columns, make certain that there are no more than 7 or 8 in the VERY IMPORTANT pile. If there are, we would suggest that you are not discriminating finely enough between the things that are important to you and we would encourage you to discriminate further.

- If there are some important values for you not represented on the cards create your own extra cards and add them to the sorting task.

- Rank-order your VERY IMPORTANT cards from the most to the least important.

- Look at the MY PAID WORK VALUES chart on page 41 and write in your rank-ordered VERY IMPORTANT work values in the left hand column.

- Write in your NOT IMPORTANT cards in the space provided.

You now have a tool you can use to analyse the suitability of any paid work prospect including your present job if you have one. You will move on in a moment to analyse your UNPAID WORK VALUES.

OF SOME
IMPORTANCE

NOT
IMPORTANT

QUITE
IMPORTANT

VERY
IMPORTANT

IMPORTANT

PLACE OF WORK
It is important that you work in the
right part of the country for you

PEACE
You prefer to have few pressures or
uncomfortable demands.

VARIETY
You enjoy having lots of different
things to do.

COMPETITION
You enjoy competing against other
people or groups.

33

INDEPENDENCE
You like being able to work in the way you want,
without others telling you what to do.

BEING

HAVING

BEING

TIME FREEDOM

You prefer to be able to choose your own times for doing things, not having rigid working hours.

FRIENDSHIP

You would or do like close friendships with people at work.

FAST PACE

You enjoy working rapidly at a high pace.

STATUS

You enjoy being in a position which leads others to respect you.

MAKING DECISIONS

It is important to you to have to make decisions about how things should be done, who should do it and when it should be done

CREATIVITY

Thinking up new ideas and ways of doing things is important to you.

RISK

You like to take risks.

EXCITEMENT

It is important to you to have a lot of excitement in your work.

MONEY

Earning a large amount of money is important to you

HELPING OTHERS

It is important to you to help other people either individually or in groups, as part of your work

DOING

DOING

BEING

BEING

HAVING

A WELL-KNOWN ORGANISATION	PROMOTION
You Like being part of a well-known organisation.	You like to work where there is a good chance of promotion.
CHALLENGE You enjoy being 'stretched' and given new problems to work on.	**ROUTINE** You like a work routine which is fairly predictable
PRESSURE You like working to dead-lines	**COMMUNITY** It is important that you work in the right part of the country for you
WORK WITH OTHERS You like to work in a team alongside others.	**PHYSICAL CHALLENGE** You enjoy doing something that is physically demanding.
WORK ALONE You like to work on your own.	**ARTISTIC** You enjoy work involving drawing, designing, making music, making models, etc.

37

DOING

HAVING   BEING

DOING

                                          DOING

COMMUNICATION
You enjoy being able to express ideas well in writing or in speech.

RECOGNITION
You do like people to appreciate you for the work you do.

SECURITY
It is important to know your work will always be there for you.

CONTACT WITH PEOPLE
You enjoy having a lot of contact with people.

PRECISE WORK
You like working at things which involve great care and concentration.

HELP SOCIETY
You like to think that your work is producing something worthwhile for society.

SUPERVISION
You enjoy being responsible for work done by others.

PERSUADING PEOPLE
You enjoy persuading people to buy something or change their minds about something.

LEARNING
It is important for you to learn new things.

BEING EXPERT
You like being known as someone with special knowledge or skills.

DOING

DOING   HAVING

BEING

DOING   BEING

Looking at your present paid work

Ask yourself this question about each of your very important work values:

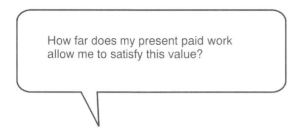

How far does my present paid work allow me to satisfy this value?

If your present paid work totally satisfies that value, you can give it 10 points.

If that value is never satisfied in that job, you award it 0 points.

Please use the full range from 0-10.

Fill in your scores in the space shown ___ on the chart below.

You will see that a weighting of your answers has already been filled in for you. Simply complete the calculations. For example:

__6__ x 8 = 48

__8__ x 7 = 56

__2__ x 6 = 12, and so on.

(The columns for Paid Work Alternatives are explained on the next page.)

MY PAID WORK VALUES			
VERY IMPORTANT	**MY PRESENT PAID WORK**	**PAID WORK ALTERNATIVE No. 1**	**PAID WORK ALTERNATIVE No. 2**
1	___ x 8 =	___ x 8 =	___ x 8 =
2	___ x 7 =	___ x 7 =	___ x 7 =
3	___ x 6 =	___ x 6 =	___ x 6 =
4	___ x 5 =	___ x 5 =	___ x 5 =
5	___ x 4 =	___ x 4 =	___ x 4 =
6	___ x 3 =	___ x 3 =	___ x 3 =
7	___ x 2 =	___ x 2 =	___ x 2 =
8	___ x 1 =	___ x 1 =	___ x 1 =
	TOTAL	TOTAL	TOTAL

My NOT IMPORTANT cards are:

1

2

3

4

5

6

7

8

Tick any of these if they feature in your present paid work or any paid work alternatives

Add up the total for your present job. If you give 10 points for each of your 8 VERY IMPORTANT values your maximum total would be 360, although it is highly unlikely that anyone would achieve 360.

Answer the following questions for yourself:

> How much opportunity is there overall in my paid work for me to find expression for those values? Do any of the values in my NOT IMPORTANT column feature in my paid work? Do I find opportunities to satisfy my values outside of my job?

> Can I think of any paid work other than my present one which would closely fit my key values? Are my work values different now than at other times in my life? In what way? Can I think of any objectives I would like to set myself as a result of this exercise?

Looking at options for alternative paid work

This part of the exercise applies if you don't have paid work and want to find some, or if you have paid work but are actively considering other options. In this case, complete the exercise by filling in your answers for as many alternative paid work options as you are considering. Total up the scores for each option separately, scoring each one on how it might provide an outlet for your work values.

> How do the alternative options compare in the scoring? Does this feel right? If not, why not?
>
> Do any of the options contain any of the NOT IMPORTANT characteristics?

> Do I need additional information before making a choice? If so, what information?
>
> Do I need to set myself any objectives?

> **Keep a record**
> - My paid work values chart
> - Notes about what I've discovered
> - Objectives I should pursue

'If work were such a good thing, the rich would have found a way of keeping it all to themselves.'
Haitian proverb

Exercise 4: What I think about unpaid work.*

- List examples of the kinds of UNPAID WORK that you do in your life on the chart My Unpaid Work Values'

  For example: cleaning the house, baby-sitting, church duties, 'do-it-yourself' activities, gardening, cooking, keeping accounts for a social club, organising outings for old people, washing clothes, etc.

- Sort the cards into columns under the 5 headings by asking yourself the question:

> What is important to me in UNPAID WORK?

- Rank order them.
- Write down your VERY IMPORTANT and NOT IMPORTANT cards.
- Use the MY UNPAID WORK VALUES CHART on page 43 – write in the activities you wish to analyse.

> How do my UNPAID WORK activities compare in the scoring? Does this feel right? If not, why not? Do any of my UNPAID WORK activities contain any of my NOT IMPORTANT values? Do I need to set myself any objectives?

> **Keep a record**
> - My unpaid work values chart
> - Notes about what I've discovered
> - Objectives I should pursue

MY UNPAID WORK VALUES

VERY IMPORTANT	ACTIVITY No. 1	ACTIVITY No. 2	ACTIVITY No. 3	ACTIVITY No. 4
1	___ x 8 =	___ x 8 =	___ x 8 =	___ x 8 =
2	___ x 7 =	___ x 7 =	___ x 7 =	___ x 7 =
3	___ x 6 =	___ x 6 =	___ x 6 =	___ x 6 =
4	___ x 5 =	___ x 5 =	___ x 5 =	___ x 5 =
5	___ x 4 =	___ x 4 =	___ x 4 =	___ x 4 =
6	___ x 3 =	___ x 3 =	___ x 3 =	___ x 3 =
7	___ x 2 =	___ x 2 =	___ x 2 =	___ x 2 =
8	___ x 1 =	___ x 1 =	___ x 1 =	___ x 1 =
	TOTAL	TOTAL	TOTAL	TOTAL

My NOT IMPORTANT cards are:

1

2

3   Tick any of these if they feature in your
            unpaid work alternatives
4

5

6

7

8

Exercise 5: Comparing what I want from paid and unpaid work.*

- Compare the results of Exercise 3 and Exercise 4 and answer the following questions:

> Are there any differences between my VERY IMPORTANT cards for PAID and UNPAID work? What are they?
>
> Any differences between my NOT IMPORTANT cards for PAID and UNPAID work?

- Make a note of the differences you observe.

- You might like to compare your analysis with that of Bill Charlton, a participant on one of our workshops, on page 45.

Keep a record

- Notes about what I've discovered.

Exercise 6: What I want from play and leisure.*

- Do the card-sort again, this time asking yourself:

> What is important to me when I play and in my leisure activities?

- Write down the 8 most important play values in the spaces provide on the MY PLAY VALUES chart below.

- Write down your 4 favourite play or leisure activities in the spaces provided.

- Ask yourself for each activity how far your play values are being satisfied (10 = totally, 0 = never)

- Write in your NOT IMPORTANT play values on the chart.

N.B. Not all of the cards will fit for PLAY, eg, promotion and place of work. Some others require translation eg, Work alone = being alone, Precise work = precise activities.

Reading only the card heading, eg, SECURITY, might be more helpful than the explanations, as many of these are specifically linked to jobs.

Keep a record

- What I've discovered about my values

MY PLAY VALUES				
VERY IMPORTANT	**PLAY No. 1**	**PLAY No. 2**	**PLAY No. 3**	**PLAY No. 4**
1	___ x 8 =	___ x 8 =	___ x 8 =	___ x 8 =
2	___ x 7 =	___ x 7 =	___ x 7 =	___ x 7 =
3	___ x 6 =	___ x 6 =	___ x 6 =	___ x 6 =
4	___ x 5 =	___ x 5 =	___ x 5 =	___ x 5 =
5	___ x 4 =	___ x 4 =	___ x 4 =	___ x 4 =
6	___ x 3 =	___ x 3 =	___ x 3 =	___ x 3 =
7	___ x 2 =	___ x 2 =	___ x 2 =	___ x 2 =
8	___ x 1 =	___ x 1 =	___ x 1 =	___ x 1 =
	TOTAL	TOTAL	TOTAL	TOTAL

My NOT IMPORTANT cards are:

1

2

3   Tick any of these if they feature in your
     play alternatives

4

5

6

7

8

Bill Charlton

Paid and Unpaid Work Values

(Example from Lifeskills workshop)

PAID WORK

VERY IMPORTANT	IMPORTANT	QUITE IMPORTANT	OF SOME IMPORTANCE	NOT IMPORTANT
Independence	Artistic	Help society	Work alone	Precise work
Creativity	Well-known	Variety	Promotion	Routine
Money	organisation	Place of work	Contact with people	Community
Communication	Fast pace	Challenge	Pressure	Physical challenge
Learning	Recognition	Risk	Competition	Security
Friendship	Making decisions	Status	Being expert	Peace
Excitement	Supervision	Persuading people		
Time freedom		Helping others		
		Work with others		

UNPAID WORK

VERY IMPORTANT	IMPORTANT	QUITE IMPORTANT	OF SOME IMPORTANCE	NOT IMPORTANT
Creativity	Work with others	Physical challenge	Contact with people	Community
Communication	Money	Peace	Being expert	Routine
Artistic	Status	Work alone	Making decisions	Promotion
Helping others		Learning	Persuading people	Supervision
Friendship		Help society	Risk	Fast pace
Time freedom		Challenge	Precise work	Recognition
Independence		Variety	Excitement	Security
Place of work				Competition
				Well-known
				organisation
				Pressure

Bill said,
'From this example it is clear that I have some values which are important to me for any work I do, whether paid or unpaid – creativity, independence, friendship, time freedom, communication. This exercise highlights just how crucial these needs are to me as a total person.

'I know what my overriding work needs are. I also know that my unpaid work needs to compensate for what I don't require as much from my paid work, e.g. artistic and physical challenge.'

Bill Charlton

Play Values

(Example from Lifeskills workshop)

PLAY VALUES

VERY IMPORTANT	IMPORTANT	QUITE IMPORTANT	OF SOME IMPORTANCE	NOT IMPORTANT
Independence	Variety	Friendship	Contact with people	Pressure
Peace	Excitement	Artistic	Precise activities	Being expert
Place	Communication	Competition	Community	Supervision
Creativity	Routine	Security	Help society	Making decisions
Physical challenge	Recognition	Challenge	Helping others	Well-known
Being alone	Fast pace	Being with others		organisation
Time freedom				Persuading people
Learning				Status
				Money

Bill said,

'This again underlines my central need for independence, creativity and time freedom in all I do. It also shows how a balance between work and play is important to me, i.e. I enjoy physical challenge and competition when playing squash and other games. I also want status, money, decision-making, supervision and persuading people to have no place in my play activities.

'There is also a contrast in that my play activities must encompass both peace and physical challenge, which for me means lying in the sun reading and a hard game of squash.

'Doing the exercise made me realise just how little time I had in my life for play and that is a thought for the AHA! folder.'

VALUES DO CHANGE

Our values are a mirror image of who we are at any moment. Perhaps more dramatically we would argue that we are merely the mirror images of our values – so central are they as the 'drivers' behind our life journeys. Periodically, however, those journeys change directions – as a result of life events, growing older, and our changing views of ourselves. There is nothing unusual about that. On the contrary, there would be something more unusual if our values stayed constant.

Exercise 7: My changing values

RAINBOW BUILDING SKILL: *Knowing yourself*
                                      Learning from experience

You have already sorted the values cards for what is important to you now. Do the following additional card sorts for paid work only.

- Sort them as you might have done when you were 18 years old.
- Sort them as if you were 30.
- Sort them as if you were 45.
- Sort them as if you were 65.

For some of these sortings you will be projecting into the future. In this context consider the following questions:

> What changes am I aware of? What do these say about me?
>
> What has stayed constant? What does this say about me?
>
> What does this say about how I see my future?

(Record this in your AHA! Folder. It will be useful data for QUESTION 3: WHAT CHANGES DO I WANT?)

Values and needs also change as a result of how successful we are in satisfying them!

Let us illuminate that curious statement. Abraham Maslow was an American psychologist who said that we must view human needs in a hierarchical way. By that he meant that our needs can be arranged in an order, some of which have be be satisfied before we can or want to address ourselves to a higher level of needs.

The diagram demonstrates this. From this it is clear that if your main concern is getting an income just to keep yourself alive, you are unlikely to be spending much time wondering about the cosmic importance of your place in the universe!

It also follows that at certain periods of your life you may revert to a lower level of need, for example, on being suddenly made redundant, or losing a spouse or partner.

Again, this re-adjustment of your needs should not in itself be a cause for concern. This reaction is a normal response to events such as these. It does not mean that in some way you have regressed.

> **Keep a record**
>
> - Notes about what I've discovered.

Self-actualisation
Creative, using full potential, determiner of own life

Self-esteem
Recognition, feeling worthwhile, respected

Belonging
Love, acceptance, being part of a group

Safety
Protection from threat and danger, security

Physiological
Food, water, shelter

Maslow's Hierarchy of Needs

Looking At Your Needs

RAINBOW BUILDING SKILL: Knowing yourself

> **Data needed**
> • Your list of VERY IMPORTANT cards from Exercises 3 & 4

Our values, simply, are an expression of our needs. This exercise will give you an opportunity to discover where you are on Maslow's levels of needs diagram. One thing you will discover is that you are unlikely to find that you are living totally at one level of need.

On the back of some of the Work Values cards are printed the following words:

HAVING   DOING   BEING

These cards represent examples of the needs in the hierarchy. Our physiological and safety needs can be grouped together as indicating things we HAVE to have before we can focus on anything else.

Our belonging and self-esteem needs indicate what we need to DO before we feel free to begin to BE the kind of person we can be. This latter represents our self-actualization needs which is where we strive to reach our full potential, unencumbered by material and social needs.

• Look at your 8 or so VERY IMPORTANT cards . How many of them are HAVING, DOING, or BEING cards?

The following cards represent each area of need.

HAVING	DOING	BEING
Security	Work with others	Learning
Money	Community	Independence
Routine	Friendship	Creativity
Peace	Contact with people	Challenge
Recognition	Help society	
Being Expert	Risk	
	Promotion	
	Status	

• Ask yourself the following questions:

> What does my card sorting tell me about where I am on the hierarchy of needs?
>
> Am I primarily at one level or are my needs distributed throughout the levels?

> What does this say about who I am now? How might I like myself to be different?

(Record this in your AHA! Folder for use with Question 3, WHAT CHANGES DO I WANT?)

> **Keep a record**
> • Notes about what I've discovered.

48

NEEDS AND WORK SATISFACTIONS

The diagram below sums up what we have been discussing about levels of needs and has an important idea added to it, developed from an American behavioural scientist, Frederick Herzberg.

Although originally concerned with paid work only, we believe his theory can apply to unpaid work too. He discovered that what made employees dissatisfied was not always the opposite of what brought them satisfaction. For example, he found that people could get very dissatisfied with problems about:

salary
job security
supervisor behaviour
company policy

but when these were rectified it did not automatically guarantee satisfaction. That only derived from factors present in the job, for example:

achievement
recognition
growth.

Herzberg called the first group 'HYGIENE' factors, because they helped to prevent dissatisfaction but in themselves would never provide real satisfaction. In other words, you can be getting a good salary in a secure job in a company you like and not feel dissatisfied, but not feel satisfied either. For that you need some of the 'MOTIVATOR' elements to be present. This can help to explain to people why sometimes they feel something is missing in their working lives yet they appear to have 'a good job'.

In short, HYGIENE factors can prevent dissatisfaction but only MOTIVATORS can guarantee satisfaction.

Exercise 9: What are my hygiene and motivation factors?

RAINBOW BUILDING SKILL: Knowing yourself

Some researchers have criticized Herzberg saying that it is naive to assume that what is a motivator for one person will be a motivator for everyone, for example, increasing responsibility. We believe strongly that although this criticism might be true it need not take away from the value of the theory. This exercise will enable you to work out for yourself what are your own HYGIENE and MOTIVATOR factors.

• Sort through the Work Values cards. Ask yourself these 2 questions:

(a) 'Which of these causes me irritation or frustration if I don't have them?'

(b) 'Which of these when I do have them makes me feel really fulfilled and involved with my work? Now sort the cards into 2 piles, according to your answers.

• Write down your answers from your cards.

List (a) represents YOUR Hygiene factors
List (b) represents YOUR Motivator factors

Does this suggest anything for my AHA! Folder?

Keep a record

• Notes about what I've discovered.

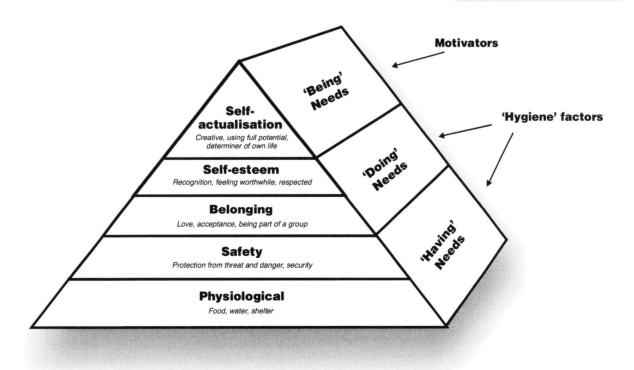

49

Rainbow Building Progress Check

WHO AM I?

What have you learned about your values and needs and how they might change?

....

....

....

....

....

....

....

....

....

....

....

....

Having looked at what is important to you (your 'values'), the next question is focused on what you can do well – your abilities or skills.

In our experience many people have difficulty in identifying their skills. Part of this difficulty reflects being brought up in a culture which deals harshly with people who brag, are immodest, or are 'too big for their boots'. Because of this, many people are more skilled in describing what they are poor at, than what they are good at! But, culture not withstanding, we are also not skilled at knowing how to identify the broad range of things we can do well. This is a vital career planning skill. It is essential to know the base of skills on which changes in your lifestyle or career could be built in the future.

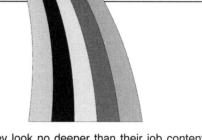

Importance of Transferable Skills

One of the reasons why we may be poor at identifying our skills can be traced to the paramount importance of the paid worker role in our lives. Skills are often linked to the jobs we do. Because we are technicians, accountants, social workers, etc., we find it relatively easy to see that we have skills in working with switch-gear, or knowledge of book-keeping systems, or an understanding of how court-orders should be followed up. However, it is often more difficult to dig deeper than these job content skills to discover the underlying skills which are transferable – not only to a variety of other jobs, but also to other life roles.

For example, many of us may have been, albeit temporarily and a long time ago, a waiter or waitress. But it would not be unusual to hear someone who had actually been a waiter for much of his or her working life, when asked what they can do, reply with a statement like 'I've only been a waiter'. This is because they look no deeper than their job content skills. In the table below, we see the job content skills for a waiter in the left-hand column and the underlying transferable skills in the other columns defined under Data, People, Things and Ideas.

We chose, for this example, the job of a waiter because it seems like a relatively straightforward job and yet it can convey, quite simply, the idea of what we are looking for in this exercise.

Certainly, a close awareness of the transferable skills involved in the jobs/roles you have been doing might alert you to other work you would be equipped to do.

SKILLS				
'None – I've only been a waiter...'†				
JOB CONTENT SKILLS	**WORKING WITH DATA**	**WORKING WITH PEOPLE**	**WORKING WITH THINGS**	**WORKING WITH IDEAS**
Setting tables			Manipulating items rapidly	Thinking of new table layouts
Seating people		Making people feel welcome		
Taking orders	Explaining menu items. Writing clearly to be understood by others	Helping		
Delivering orders to kitchen	Communicating information to others	Checking for understanding; maintain relationships		Thinking of new systems for dealing with orders
Serving food	Ability to memorise		Balancing items	
Suggesting desserts	Ability to memorise		Being persuasive	
Checking on satisfaction	Seeking feedback	Listening, caring		
Delivering bill, taking money and providing change	Copying; numeracy	Dealing with people courteously		
Thanking customers		Dealing with people courteously		

† Freely adapted from Richard Bolles, *The Three Boxes of Life*, Berkeley, Ten Speed Press.

RAINBOW BUILDING SKILLS: ***Knowing yourself***
Research skills

On the following pages headed 'SKILLS DESCRIPTIONS' you will find a number of cards to cut out, as you did for the Work Values exercise.

• Amongst the cards you cut out will be 4 cards with the following words on them:

VERY COMPETENT

COMPETENT

ADEQUATE FOR TASK

UNDEVELOPED

• Place these 4 cards in front of you. Sort all the rest under them by asking yourself:

> Which of these skills can I perform very competently, competently, adequately, and which have I not yet developed?

• If you believe you have some transferable skills which are not represented on the cards, write these on the blank cards provided.

• Write down in the table on page 59 all the skills at which you assess yourself as VERY COMPETENT and COMPETENT.

• Look at the skills in the COMPETENT, ADEQUATE, and UNDEVELOPED columns. At which of these would you like to become more competent? Write these down in the table.

• Take your VERY COMPETENT and COMPETENT skills and sort them into 3 piles indicating those you:

– WANT TO USE A GREAT DEAL

– WANT TO USE SOMETIMES

– WANT TO USE RARELY OR NEVER

The skills you have identified as your VERY COMPETENT ones and WANT TO USE A GREAT DEAL are your most transferable skills.

The skills you have identified as your COMPETENT and WANT TO USE A GREAT DEAL are your next most transferable skills.

Not wanting to use these skills does not necessarily make them non-transferable. But we have found that people are less likely to want to look for opportunities which involve using skills they are less motivated to use.

Data, Ideas, People, Things

For the next part of the exercise, note that each of the skill cards has a letter on them: D, I, P or T – standing for Data, Ideas, People and Things.

D = DATA. These cards represent the kind of skills required to record, communicate, evaluate, and organise facts or data about goods and services. People who like using these skills typically enjoy working with figures, systems, and routines.

I = IDEAS. These represent skills used in being creative. designing conceptual models and systems, experimenting with words, figures, music. People who like using these skills typically enjoy creating, discovering, interpreting, synthesising and abstract thinking.

P = PEOPLE. These represent skills used in helping, informing, teaching, serving, persuading, entertaining, motivating, selling and directing other people. People with these skills generally like to engage in work with a great deal of interaction with others.

T = THINGS. These represent skills used in making, repairing, transporting, servicing, using equipment or carrying out technical tasks. People with these skills like using tools and machinery and understanding how things work.

> How many of my transferable skills are in each of the categories - DATA, IDEAS, PEOPLE or THINGS?

• Add these letters to the table on page 59 which lists your transferable skills. Place D, I, P or T after each skill.

VERY COMPETENT	COMPETENT	ADEQUATE FOR TASK
UNDEVELOPED	p Drawing out people	T Hand–eye co-ordination
T Keeping physically fir	T Using hand tools	T Handling things with precision and speed
T Assembling things	T Fixing, repairing things	D Analysing, dissecting, sorting and sifting through information or things
T Building, constructing	T Muscular co-ordination	D Problem-solving
T Finding out how things work	T Physically strong	D Reviewing, evaluating
T Driving car, motorbike	T Quick physical reactions	D Diagnosing, looking for problems
T Manual dexterity	T Using machine tools, sewing machine, lathe, power tools	D Organising, classifying

D Reading for facts	D Following instructions, diagrams, blueprints	I Creating, innovating, seeing alternatives
D Researching, gathering information	I Working creatively with colours	I Sizing up a situation or person quickly and accurately
D Manipulating numbers rapidly in mental arithmetic	I Conveying feelings or thoughts through drawing, painting, etc.	T Handling things with precision and speed
D Calculating, computing	I Fashioning or shaping things or materials	I Reading for ideas
D Memorising numbers	I Working creatively with spaces, shapes or faces	I Developing others' ideas
D Managing money, budgeting	I Composing music	I Conveying feelings or thoughts through body, face and/or voice
D Examining, observing, surveying; an eye for detail and accuracy	I Improvising, adapting	I Writing creatively
D Taking an inventory	I Designing things, events, learning situations	P Conveying warmth and caring

P Helping others	P Taking first move in relationships	P Promoting change
P Giving credit to others, showing appreciation	P Motivating people	P Leading, directing others
P Listening	P Organising people	P Showing sensitivity to others' feelings
P Selling, persuading, negotiating	P Teaching, training	P Performing in a group, on stage, in public, etc.

MY TRANSFERABLE SKILLS			
VERY COMPETENT	COMPETENT	WANT TO USE A GREAT DEAL	SKILLS I WOULD LIKE TO DEVELOP
		WANT TO USE SOMETIMES	
		WANT TO USE RARELY OR NEVER	

Job Families

If you look at the World of Employment Map below you will see that all areas of employment are located there. Jobs have been assigned to 24 Job Families. A Job Family is a group of jobs related to one another on the basis of their degree of involvement in working with Data, Ideas, People and Things. The 24 Job Families are described in Appendix 1 (page 153).

Each Job Family is located on the World of Employment Map according to how alike it is to the other 23 Job Families when compared according to Data, Ideas, People and Things. The map is split into 12 regions. Those regions next to one another have most in common. Those on opposite sides of the circle have least in common.

If you have transferable skills primarily in:

People:	you might explore jobs in	*Regions 12 & 1*
People & Data:	you might explore jobs in	*Region 2*
Data:	you might explore jobs in	*Regions 3 & 4*
Data & Things:	you might explore jobs in	*Region 5*
Things:	you might explore jobs in	*Regions 6 & 7*
Things & Ideas:	you might explore jobs in	*Region 8*
Ideas:	you might explore jobs in	*Regions 9 & 10*
Ideas & People:	you might explore jobs in	*Region 11*

For a more direct reading of which jobs might be suitable for you according to your interests, look up a specific Job Family in Appendix 1.Families are arranged in alphabetical order,and are subdivided into broad job groupings which in turn list specific jobs.

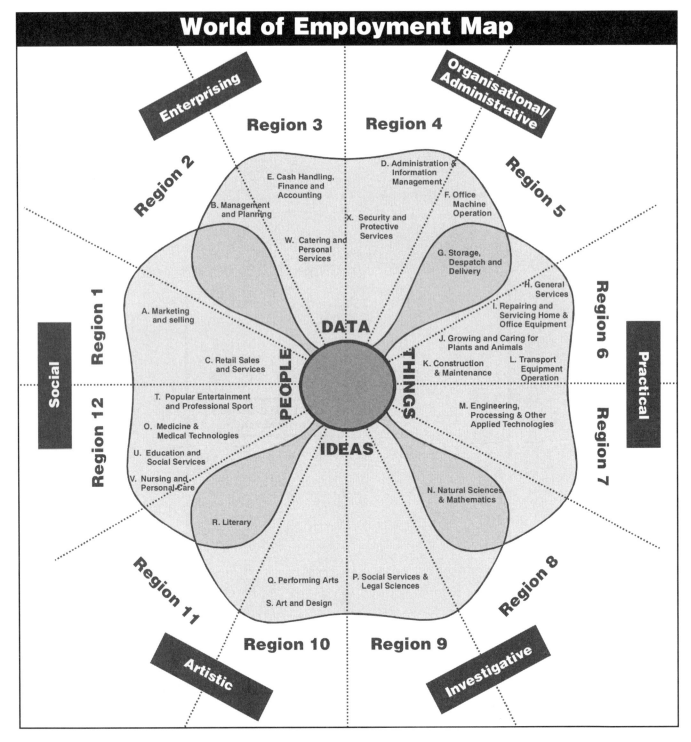

Each Job Family also includes a range of courses that require similar skills or that attract people with similar interests. See the World of Education Map below and Appendix 3 to identify education courses that might correspond to your skills and interests.

Moira Dalgleish

(Example from Lifeskills workshop)

Moira's skills were primarily in Ideas. The World of Employment Map on page 60 suggests that she would be able to use those skills most in Regions 9 and 10. In those regions are found Job Families: Q, P, and S. She looked these up in Appendix 1, having first identified her qualifications level as 2. None of these jobs appealed greatly to her so she looked at the next closest Job Families, which were R and N. Out of those N was of the most interest because her next highest group of skills was in THINGS.

This does *not* mean that Moira must look for a job in these areas. It does mean that with the skills that she has she is most likely to be able to adapt to the skill demands of these jobs.

From the next exercise, however, we shall discover that she has interests which do not coincide exactly with her skills.

World of Education Map

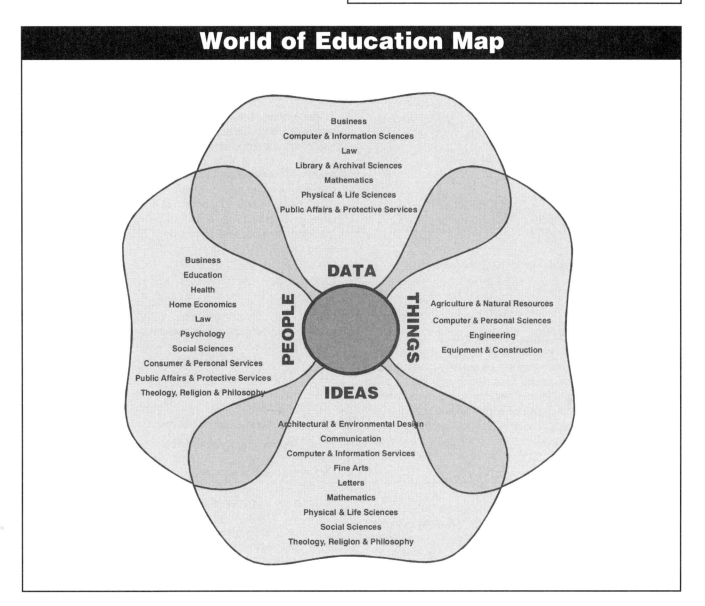

Looking at Your Interests

RAINBOW BUILDING SKILL: Knowing yourself

Your interests represent your preferences for doing some activities instead of others. Some people like driving cars, others like exploring caves, some like keeping financial records, while others like drawing diagrams.

This exercise is based on the work of John Holland[8] who discovered that people's interests incline them to particular types of occupation. He also found that people in the same occupation, although they may have different values, will have similar skills and interests.

- On the next page are 6 sets of statements. For each of them, show how much you agree or disagree with the statement.

> 1 = Highly disagree
> 5 = Highly agree

Circle the number that represents your level of agreement.

- Rank order the letters P, I, A, S, E, and O/A according to which interest group has the highest and the lowest scores for you.

- Take your top 3 scores. These represent your 3 major interest types.

My top group is.........................
My second highest group is.................
My third highest group is...............................

There follows an interpretation for each interest group.

Interest Types

PRACTICAL: THINGS FOCUS

These people like to work with tools, objects, machines or animals. They like to develop manual, mechanical, agricultural and electronic skills. They like jobs which involve building and repairing things. They like using their hands. They use their bodies skillfully rather than words, thoughts or feelings. They admire physical co-ordination, strength, agility and logic. They like being outdoors and dealing with concrete problems. They tend to be down to earth and matter of fact. They solve problems by DOING.

INVESTIGATIVE: IDEAS FOCUS

These people enjoy using their minds. They tend to be curious, studious, independent, intellectual, sometimes unconventional, and introspective. They like to develop skills in maths, biology and the physical sciences. They like scientific and medical jobs. They like thinking through problems, trusting their own minds more than other people and things. They admire logic, use insight, enjoy intellectual challenges. They solve problems by THINKING.

ARTISTIC: IDEAS AND PEOPLE FOCUS

These people like to feel free from routine. They like to develop skills in language, art, music, drama and writing. They trust their minds, bodies and feelings, being more suspicious of things. They enjoy beauty, unstructured activity, variety, interesting and unusual sounds, sights, textures and people. They tend to be creative, talented and freewheeling, often non-conformist, sensitive, independent, introspective, expressive. They like jobs where they can use their creative skills. They solve problems by being CREATIVE.

SOCIAL: PEOPLE FOCUS

These people live through their feelings. Relying on gut reactions, they like activities that involve informing, training, teaching, understanding and helping others. They develop skills for working with people. They tend to be helpful, friendly, concerned leaders, sensitive, supportive, responsible, perceptive, genuine, tactful, empathetic. They enjoy being close to people, sharing problems, being in charge, unstructured activities. They like jobs such as teaching, nursing, and counselling. They solve problems by using their FEELINGS.

ENTERPRISING: PEOPLE AND DATA FOCUS

These people love projects. They like leading and influencing people, are often ambitious, outgoing, energetic, self-confident, independent, enthusiastic, sensitive and logical. They develop skills to lead, motivate and persuade people. They enjoy organising, managing, variety, status, power and money. They solve problems, by RISKING themselves and others.

ORGANISATIONAL/ADMINISTRATIVE: DATA AND THINK FOCUS

These people enjoy orderliness and clear routines. They like activities that encourage organising information in a clear and logical way. They tend to be responsible, dependable, careful, logical, and accurate. They have an eye for detail. They enjoy order, security and certainty, identifying with power and status. They develop office and arithmetical skills. They like jobs involving systems, operating computers and word processors. They often like working in large organisations. They solve problems by following ROUTINES.

Analysis of Interests

INTERESTS – GROUP P (Practical)

1 2 3 4 5   I like fixing and repairing things

1 2 3 4 5   I liketo be very fit

1 2 3 4 5   I like making things with my hands

1 2 3 4 5   I like doing things outdoors

1 2 3 4 5   I like hard, physical work

1 2 3 4 5   I feel comfortable working with tools and machines

Add up the numbers   TOTAL FOR P =

INTERESTS – GROUP I (Ideas)

1 2 3 4 5   I like to understand things thoroughly

1 2 3 4 5   I like exploring new ideas

1 2 3 4 5   I enjoy working on problems

1 2 3 4 5   I like asking questions

1 2 3 4 5   I like learning about new things

1 2 3 4 5   I like to work out my own answers to problems

Add up the numbers   TOTAL FOR I =

INTERESTS – GROUP A (Artistic)

1 2 3 4 5   I like seeing art shows, plays and good films

1 2 3 4 5   I like to be different

1 2 3 4 5   I like to forget about everything else when I'm being creative

1 2 3 4 5   It is vital to have beautiful and unusual things around me

1 2 3 4 5   I like to use my imagination

1 2 3 4 5   I like expressing myself on paper, through painting, music, or by building things

Add up the numbers   TOTAL FOR A =

INTERESTS – GROUP S (Social)

1 2 3 4 5   I enjoy being with people

1 2 3 4 5   I like to talk things through with people

1 2 3 4 5   I like to pay attention to what people want

1 2 3 4 5   I like helping people

1 2 3 4 5   I like helping people to develop and learn things

1 2 3 4 5   Who I'm with is more important than where I am

Add up the numbers   TOTAL FOR S =

INTERESTS – GROUP E (Enterprising)

1 2 3 4 5   I enjoy trying to persuade and influence people

1 2 3 4 5   I enjoy using a great deal of energy and resilience

1 2 3 4 5   I like people to do what I ask of them

1 2 3 4 5   I liketaking risks

1 2 3 4 5   I like making decisions

1 2 3 4 5   I enjoy getting people organised and excited about a task

Add up the numbers   TOTAL FOR E =

INTERESTS – GROUP O/A

1 2 3 4 5   I like to be given clear directions

1 2 3 4 5   I enjoy getting the details right in my work

1 2 3 4 5   I like a clear structure and a regular routine

1 2 3 4 5   I can be relied upon to do what I'm expected to do

1 2 3 4 5   I enjoy working with figures

1 2 3 4 5   I like organising projects, ideas and people down to the last detail

Add up the numbers   TOTAL FOR O/A =

- Examine the World of Employment Map on page 60. You will see that each interest type corresponds to 2 regions.

Practical	=	Regions 6 and 7
Investigative	=	Regions 8 and 9
Artistic	=	Regions 10 and 11
Social	=	Regions 12 and 1
Enterprising	=	Regions 2 and 3
Organisational/ Administrative	=	Regions 4 and 5

- Put an X in the regions which incorporate your top 3 letters (P, I, A, S, E or O/A).

  These represent the Job Families where people with your kind of interest tend to cluster.

- For a more direct reading of which jobs might be suitable for you according to your interests, look up your 3-letter code in Appendix 2 (page 169). There you will find Job Family regions classified according to the 3-letter codes. Look at Appendix 1 (page 153). Find the Job Families indicated from your 3-letter code, decide on your Level of Entry, and see which jobs match your interests.

Choosing a leisure pursuit

- Using your primary interest areas, as determined in the first part of this Exercise, check to see the kinds of activity that are typical for people with your interests profile in Appendix 4 (page 177).

- Enter your 10 favourite leisure time activities in the table opposite in rank order from your most favourite to your 10th favourite. Include any that you would like to try but may not have tried yet in your life.

- The other columns in the table ask you to fill in details about the selected leisure activities – for example, can you do it alone or do you need others, does it cost you money, is it energetic, is it risking in any way, etc. Ask yourself the following question:

> What does this say about your leisure life?

For example, on one of our workshops, Kate discovered that she needed a balance of activities involving people and being alone. Dave was not surprised to find a high level of physical risk in his activities (he scored high on Practical and Enterprising). Linda found she rarely did any of the things she enjoyed doing. Jacob realised that his leisure activities cost him almost nothing and Margaret his wife, found 3 activities from Appendix 3 that she had never thought of doing but had now included in her list.

Moira Dalgleish

(Example from Lifeskills workshop)

Moira's 3-letter code was S,I,O/A, Social, Investigative, and Organisational/Administrative. The Investigative interests (Regions 8 and 9) are consistent with her skills. This means that the jobs in Social Sciences and Legal Services (Q and P) and in the Natural Sciences and Mathematics (N) are likely to be ones she would be both interested in and would be able to do.

Moira's strongest interest, however, was in the Social area (Regions 12 and 1). Just because she does not possess skills which are not immediately and obviously transferable to these jobs does not mean that she should not consider them. It does mean that she needs to think extra carefully about it. But given sufficiently high motivation, people can develop skills in many areas in which they have not yet demonstrated expertise.

Her biggest contrast is between her interests in Regions 4 and 5 (Organisational/Administrative) and her skills which are primarily opposite these regions on the map, in Regions 9 and 10. Again this should not automatically rule out a job choice in Regions 4 and 5, but she would need to analyse the job specifications carefully and ask herself if she is really prepared to put in the work to develop the new skills that clearly would be called upon.

> **Watch Point**
>
> There is some evidence to suggest that our interests determine how we spend our leisure time as well as the kind of paid work we choose to do. In looking up your most likely leisure activities in Appendix 3 you should find the kinds of things that would appeal to you. However, remember that although many people have leisure interests similar to their paid work interests, some people like their leisure interests to appeal to a different aspect of their personality. John, a very successful sales manager who loves his job (Enterprising) as a complete break enjoys building model ships (Practical).

MY LEISURE ACTIVITIES						
LEISURE ACTIVITY	Alone (A) or with People (P)	Does it cost £5 or more (£)?	Does it involve risk? Physical (P) Emotional (E) Intellectual (I)	Energetic (E) or Non-energetic (NE)?	Do you do it: Often (O) Sometimes (S) Rarely (R)?	When did you last do it?
1.						
2.						
3.						
4.						
5.						
6.						
7.						
8.						
9.						
10.						

Keep a record

- The results of the interests questionnaire
- The World of Employment Map regions which correspond to My interest scores
- The Job Families which match my interests
- The leisure activities which Match my interests

Rainbow Building Progress Check

WHO AM I?

What have you learned about the types of job which would match your skills and interests?

What have you learned about leisure pursuits in which you might engage?

....
....
....
....
....
....
....
....
....
....
....
....
....
....
....
....
....
....

Choosing Where To Live

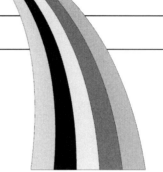

RAINBOW BUILDING SKILLS: *Knowing yourself*
                                      Research skills

In the past 50 years we have become more mobile than at any time in our history since the waves of invaders prior to 1066. People are moving home and job more frequently than ever before. Much of the movement, however, is still quite local, and as a nation we are still relatively static when we compare ourselves with the gypsy-like wanderings of the Americans. Yet the reality is that we *do* have the ability to choose where we live and work, and we should all exercise this choice positively. Remember:

RAINBOW BUILDERS ALWAYS HAVE A CHOICE

This exercise is designed to get you to reassess the choice you have and are making by living where you are now. You can choose to live elsewhere in our country. It is increasingly easy to live and work in EEC countries, and it is possible to emigrate to other countries – traditionally Australia, New Zealand, Canada, South Africa, the USA, but in theory large parts of the globe.

- On the next page you will see 15 balloons displaying 12 different aspects of location. There are 3 blank balloons for you to add any aspects important to you but missing from our list. Most of the balloons we think are self-explanatory, but perhaps an explanation of some of them would help you:

TOWN/COUNTRY = living in either a town or the country is important to you, or some combination of the two.

PROXIMITY TO FAMILY = the distance you live from relatives and in-laws.

CULTURAL AMENITIES = availability of theatre, cinema, art galleries, further educational opportunities, restaurants, libraries.

- Rank order on page 69 the balloons in the figure overleaf according to their importance to you. Your most important aspect placed alongside 15, your next most important beside 14, etc.

- Then rate each aspect according to how far that is satisfied by your present place of living by allocating it 0, 1, or 2 in the space provided.

      0 = not satisfied at all
      1 = some satisfaction
      2 = mostly or completely satisfied

- Multiply your own ranking by the rating from 0-2, as you can see in the example below. Then add up the total. This will give you an indication of how well you see your living needs are being satisfied right now. The maximum total possible is 240, the lowest total possible is 0.

FOR EXAMPLE

15. Favourable Climate	Score (0)	15 x 0 = 0
14. Town/Country	Score (2)	14 x 2 = 28
13. Clean Environment	Score (1)	13 x 1 = 13
12. Low Crime Levels	Score (1)	12 x 1 = 12

and so on...

- The following will give you some indication of what your scores mean

180-240	Well matched. Probably enjoy where you're living. Little reason to look for a change.
140-179	Quite well matched. Some things missing which will need compensating for. Not much of an incentive to move.
100-139	Adequate. You will often think about moving but probably won't.
60-90	Inadequate. This leaves much to be desired about where you live. You should seriously be questioning whether you should stay. What in particular are you not getting? Is it a widespread dissatisfaction or just related to a few outstanding absences?
Below 60	Do you really want to stay???

- You can, of course, use your rankings to compare your present living place with other places in the country to which you might consider moving.

Aspects of Location

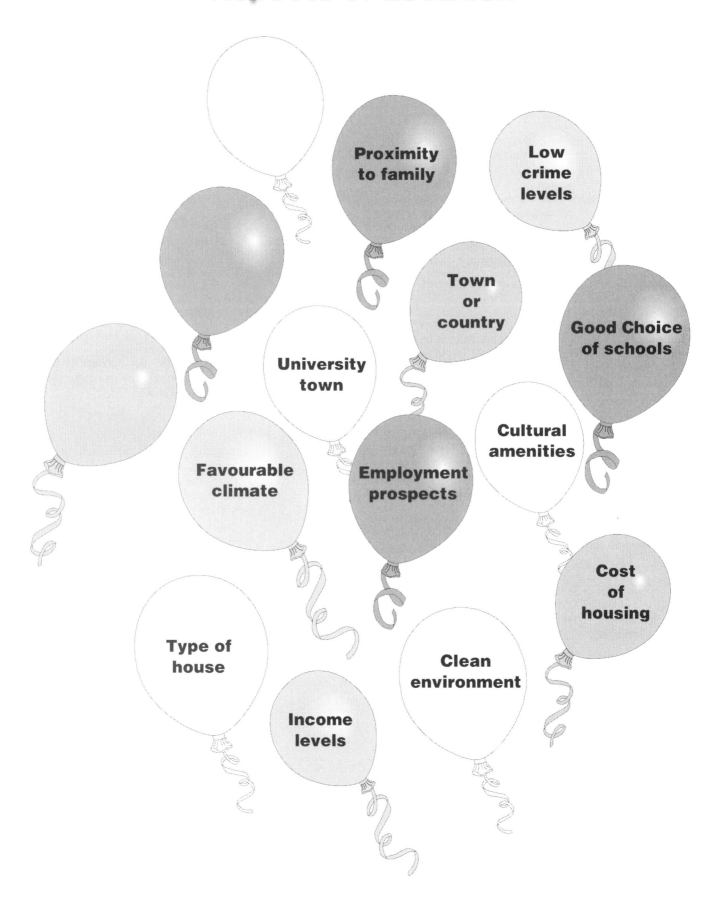

WHAT I WANT FROM WHERE I LIVE

E

(0, 1 or 2)

15. _____ 15 x_____ = _____

14. _____ 14 x_____ = _____

13. _____ 13 x_____ = _____

12. _____ 12 x_____ = _____

11. _____ 11 x_____ = _____

10. _____ 10 x_____ = _____

9. _____ 9 x_____ = _____

8. _____ 8 x_____ = _____

7. _____ 7 x_____ = _____

6. _____ 6 x_____ = _____

5. _____ 5 x_____ = _____

4. _____ 4 x_____ = _____

3. _____ 3 x_____ = _____

2. _____ 2 x_____ = _____

1. _____ 1 x_____ = _____

TOTAL POINTS =

Keep a record

- The results of the ranking and Rating exercise

- Notes about the sorts of living situation/locations which might suit you better

69

Rainbow Building Summary Sheet

WHO AM I?

My major PAID WORK VALUES are:	My major UNPAID WORK VALUES are:
_____	_____
_____	_____
_____	_____
_____	_____
_____	_____
_____	_____
_____	_____
_____	_____
_____	_____
_____	_____
_____	_____
_____	_____

My TRANSFERABLE SKILLS are in:	My major INTERESTS are in:
PEOPLE	P
DATA	I
IDEAS	A
THINGS	E
	S
(Circle)	(Circle) O/A

My major TRANSFERABLE SKILLS are:	I want to LIVE somewhere that has the following attributes (in order):
_____	_____
_____	_____
_____	_____
_____	_____
_____	_____
_____	_____
_____	_____
_____	_____
_____	_____

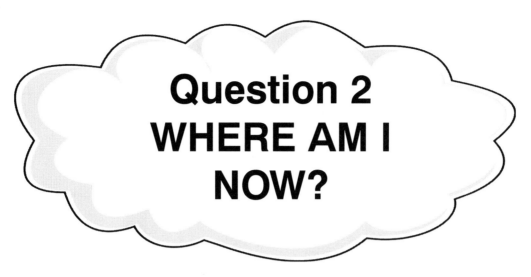

Question 2
WHERE AM I NOW?

Having identified your skills, values and interests, and knowing something about your preferred lifestyle, it is now time to stop and examine where you are on your journey through life.

ROUTE MAP
for "Where Am I Now?"

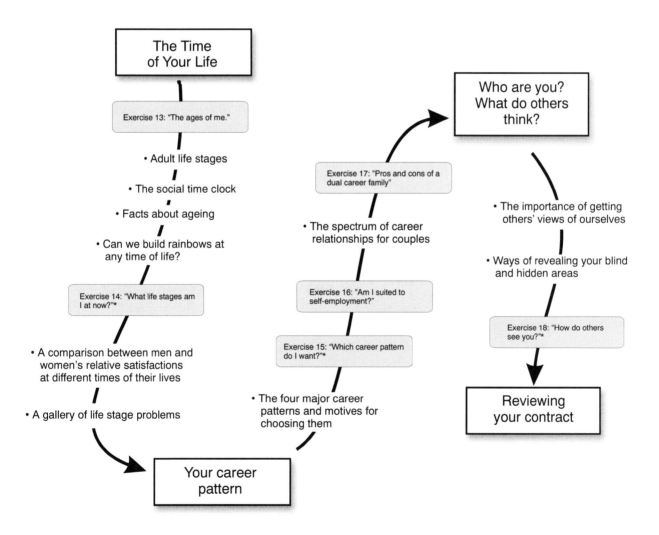

The Time
of Your Life

Exercise 13: "The ages of me."

• Adult life stages

• The social time clock

• Facts about ageing

• Can we build rainbows at
any time of life?

Exercise 14: "What life stages am
I at now?"*

• A comparison between men and
women's relative satisfactions
at different times of their lives

• A gallery of life stage problems

Your career
pattern

Exercise 17: "Pros and cons of a
dual career family"

• The spectrum of career
relationships for couples

Exercise 16: "Am I suited to
self-employment?"

Exercise 15: "Which career pattern
do I want?"*

• The four major career
patterns and motives for
choosing them

Who are you?
What do others
think?

• The importance of getting
others' views of ourselves

• Ways of revealing your blind
and hidden areas

Exercise 18: "How do others
see you?"*

Reviewing
your contract

The Time Of Your Life

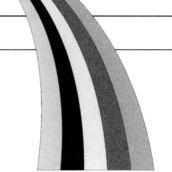

RAINBOW BUILDING SKILL: Knowing yourself

- Fill in the gaps in the following sentences

  1. In other people's eyes, I look as though I am about .... years of age.

  2. In my own eyes, I judge my body to be like that of a person of about .... years of age.

  3. My thoughts and interests are like those of a person about .... years of age.

  4. My position in society is like that of a person about .... years of age.

  5. Deep down inside, I really feel like a person about .... years of age.

And just one more question:

  6. I would honestly prefer to be about .... years of age.

> What do my answers say about me and how I see myself?
>
> What does it say about how I regard ageing?

Probably, if you are like most people, you will not have given the same age for all the questions. That is because age is so very much more than a biological process. It is highly charged with social and emotional significance.

One of the most typical differences in people's answers occurs between 'feel' and chronological ages. People in their third decade and beyond usually 'feel' younger than their 'official' age. This remains true of many people in their 70s and 80s.

It has been found that most people in their third decade and beyond prefer to be younger than their actual chronological age. Very rarely, however, do people actually express a preference for being older, except for some young teenagers.

It is tempting to shrug and say, 'Well, that is just about what we would expect, isn't it?' But why is this just what we would expect? The fact is that many people do have an aversion to old age, but ageing does not have to be a negative experience, and in many cultures is not.

†Adapted from Robert Kastenbaum, *Growing Old*, Harper & Collins

What is known about Adult life stages?

Modern developmental psychology is notorious for its preoccupation with infancy and adolescence and its neglect of adulthood. Until comparatively recently, when looking at a typical textbook in psychology, you could think that human development stopped at age 21. Fortunately, writers and philosophers have been more observant, more introspective, and less timid in exploring the longest period of our lives.

The Talmud, 2500 years ago, in the 'Sayings of the Fathers', outlined 14 ages of Man, complete with developmental tasks! In 500 BC, Confucius identified 6 steps in the life cycle, while the Greek poet Solon in 700 BC, divided life into ten stages, each lasting 7 years. More recently, and better known, Shakespeare in 'As You Like It' outlined seven ages of man.

But until the 1970s, there was almost complete silence from behavioural scientists about the experience of being adult. Daniel Levinson[9] has described the nature of adult life as 'one of the best-kept secrets in our society, and probably in human history generally'.

One of the consequences of this is that people in general have often assumed a stability in adult life which recent research has demonstrated to be the exception rather than the rule. People so quickly negate their own experience when they believe that the experience is probably unique and so the myth continues.

Yet alongside the concept of stability is a clear identification in many people's eyes of what is appropriate behaviour for one's age. In other words there is an implicit understanding of different stages of life – the experimentation of adolescence, the settling down into a job and long-term relationship, becoming parents then grandparents, and finally, retirement.

The different tasks which accompany these events are talked about, but the psychological changes concomitant with them much less so. Consequently myths develop about the different age groups, eg, young adults under 25 are supposed to be autonomous, exuberant, high in drive to achieve and be reluctant to be 'looked after'. Therefore, when 25 year old men and women find themselves apathetic, tired and depressed by the limited circumstances of their lives, they are doubly depressed – by their actual life situation plus the feeling that people of their age should not be like this. They feel they cannot ask for help from others because they are supposed to be independent. If they enjoy being quiet, low-achievers, they suspect that there must be something wrong with them.

All too often they jump into roles that they think they 'should' be ready for – deciding on a long-term career, forming relationships, having children – when clearly they are not ready.

Similarly, the myth of the middle years is that adults are responsible, settled, contented, at the peak of their achievements. But what of the adults in this group who find that instead of being content with their responsibilities they wish to explore new experiences, try new careers, new styles of living?

At 60 to 65, people are supposed to become 'old' – ready to retire, lose their health, their wits and their income, be dependent on their children, to be hopeless and unattractive. But what if they are fully fit, alert, fall in love with someone new, want a divorce, act out a lifelong ambition to travel round the world, etc?

The social time clock

Bernice Neugarten[10] has suggested that 'there exists a socially prescribed timetable for the ordering of major life events' and that most adults conform to this timetable. Remarkable agreement has been found in the general population regarding what age is appropriate for particular behaviour. For example, 4 in 5 believed that a man should marry between 20 and 25 and a woman between 19 and 24; that people should finish their education and get a job between 20 and 22; retire between 60 and 65. It is as if there is a social time clock which regulates our lives, by which we judge whether we are 'on-time' for certain things in our lives.

To be 'off-time', whether early or late, is to be an age deviant. Like any other kind of deviance, this carries with it social penalties. The woman not married by age 29 used to – and maybe still does – feel embarrassed by it. The man who returns to college at 45 can feel and be treated as peculiar. It can be as shameful to have a baby at age 45 as at age 15.

It does seem that it is harder for a person to go against age expectations in their 20s than in their 40s.

The evidence clearly suggests that there are strong culturally transmitted expectations of behaviour relating to adulthood. This makes people feel good if they are 'on-time' and bad if they are 'off-time'. But what is the empirical evidence for some of these age-bound expectations?

Changes in adulthood: The facts[11]

Physical development

The range of individual differences is enormous and no physical change during adulthood can be exactly predicted from chronological age – the one possible exception being grey hair! Longevity and youthfulness run in families and are also more class than age related. People from lower socio-economic groups tend to age faster and die sooner than those from middle and upper socio-economic groups, and to suffer from poorer health throughout their lives. There follows a list of findings:

- maximum height is attained at the beginning of adulthood;

- strength peaks between 25 and 30, after which the muscles – especially in the back and the legs – weaken somewhat unless maintained by exercise;

- manual dexterity is greatest at about 33;

- sight diminishes throughout adulthood;

- in middle age, people tend to put on weight around the waist and hips;

- there is gradual hearing loss after 20, especially among men;

- sensitivity to smell decreases at 40;

- sensitivity to taste diminishes after 50;

- appearance alters at middle age – hair greys and recedes, skin coarsens and darkens, wrinkles appear;

- adults get fewer acute illnesses and more chronic ones than children;

- older adults take longer to recuperate from illness;

- sexual potency reaches its peak in late adolescence for men and in the mid-twenties for women†

- women cease menstruation at 40-50

Intellectual development

It used to be thought by psychologists that intelligence followed an inverted U-shaped curve, peaking in the mid-20s, then declining. However, once the different dimensions of 'intelligence' are examined, the picture looks very different:

- the capacity for rapid processing of information in problem solving ('fluid intelligence') declines steadily from the late teens;

- 'crystallised intelligence' which relates to the storage of information such as vocabulary and general knowledge, increases over the adult years;

- short-term memory is variable but long-term memory remains stable, especially with practice;

- problem solving and reasoning may deteriorate slightly with age, especially when speed is called for;

- creative output varies widely according to the subject - chemists and mathematicians have tended to peak in their 20s and 30s, novelists in their 40s and 50s, poets in their 20s, architects in their late 40s.

Motivation is obviously a key factor and older people may learn more – and learn it better – because they want more intensely to learn and so work harder at it.

†Potency, of course, relates to quantity, not quality!

Can we build RAINBOWS at any stage of life?

Yes, but they will probably look very different at different stages.

We have already discussed the widespread ignorance of adult development from an empirical viewpoint until the 1970s. Then came the work of Levinson[9], Sheehy[3] and others. We have combined these studies to produce the following table.

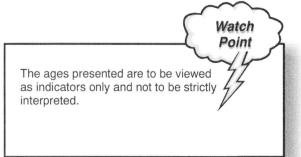

The ages presented are to be viewed as indicators only and not to be strictly interpreted.

STAGES AND TASKS OF ADULTHOOD		
STAGES	**AGES**	**TASK**
	— 16 —	
PULLING UP ROOTS		Autonomy Self-sufficiency
	— 20 —	
PROVISIONAL ADULTHOOD		Select career, make relationships Achieve place in society
	— 28 —	
AGE 30 TRANSITION		Search for identity and meaning in life Re-assess future objectives
	— 32 —	
ROOTING		Establish long-term goals, get career recognition
	— 39 —	
MID-LIFE TRANSITION		Re-examination of career and personal relationships. Assess gap between achievement and aspirations.
	— 45 —	
RESTABILISATION AND FLOWERING		Autonomy Acceptance of time as finite
	— 55 —	
MELLOWING AND RENEWAL		Acceptance of what one has Fewer personal relationships Enjoyment of here-and-now.
	— 65+ —	

RAINBOW BUILDING SKILL: Knowing yourself

- Below you will see eight sentence stems regarding various aspects of your life.

  Circle the letter (a, b, c, d, e, f, g) which you feel most accurately describes you currently as you see yourself.

Your response should be on the basis of how you think things really are, not how you would like them to be.

In some cases, more than one statement may describe your current situation. However, you are to select the one statement which is most characteristic of you.

- Enter the letters you have circled in the table overleaf.

Adult Life-Stage Questionnaire†

1. My main concern is:

- a. becoming a contributing member of my chosen profession
- b. financial security for retirement purposes
- c. being able to fend for myself
- d. accepting what I have not achieved with my life
- e. taking advantage of my last chance to make it big
- f. selecting the right career
- g. finding out what I want out of life

2. My interpersonal relationships are characterised by:

- a. turmoil and change often being caused by my wanting to find out more about myself
- b. a desire for confirmation of my life choices
- c. a lack of excitement but a need for support; achieving recognition in my career
- d. stability and a sense of well-being
- e. being less intense
- f. a need for support from my close friends
- g. a re-awakening of my old dependent-independent feelings

3. One of my dominant goals is:

- a. really enjoying the here-and-now
- b. achieving independence from my parents
- c. identifying what my life means to me and what I can do with the limited time I have left
- d. deciding what to do with my life
- e. making enough money to do what I want
- f. discovering what is right for me
- g. being active socially

4. My primary value is:

- a. security
- b. autonomy
- c. accomplishment/prestige
- d. independence
- e. self-identity
- f. commitment
- g. wisdom

5. My life is:

- a. full of urgency to succeed
- b. not so rushed; it is a time for sharing human experiences
- c. a complete open book; anything could happen
- e. stable; what has been done, has been done
- e. for me to define and control
- f. passing too quickly; I have one last chance to make it
- g. uncertain and full of crucial decisions

6. The future is:

- a. uncertain and becoming increasingly important
- b. full of possibilities
- c. pressing in on me and I am running out of opportunities
- d. not as important as the present
- e. not important
- f. a time I fantasise about
- g. limited and I feel a time squeeze

7. My career behaviour is characterised by:

- a. having conflicts between my career and other demands in my life
- b. getting my career into its proper perspective
- c. learning about the world of employment
- d. reviewing what I want from my career
- e. becoming more effective at what I do
- f. a concern for being remembered when I retire
- g. discovering my skills

8. My identity is:

- a. defined by how well I perform in my job
- b. torn between what I am now and wanting to change
- c. well-established with a feeling of relief
- d. well-defined and I am satisfied
- e. still tied up with my family
- f. well-defined even though I may not be completely satisfied with it
- g. something which I don't seem to have control of

---

†This exercise has been adapted from the Development Stage Assessment Questionnaire produced by Sperry, Michelson and Hunsaker[12]

Item	Pulling-up roots (16-20)	Provisional adulthood (20-28)	Age 30 transition (28-32)	Rooting (32-39)	Mid-life transition (39-45)	Restabilization and flowering (45-55)	Mellowing (55-65+)
1	c	f	g	a	e	d	b
2	f	b	a	c	g	d	e
3	b	d	f	e	c	g	a
4	d	f	e	c	b	a	g
5	c	e	g	a	f	d	b
6	f	b	a	g	c	d	e
7	c	g	a	e	d	b	f
8	e	f	g	a	b	c	d
Total no. of items circled in each column	_____	_____	_____	_____	_____	_____	_____

The column with the highest frequency of circled items indicates the stage of adult development most characteristic of you now. You will probably find that your scores range across many of the life stages.

What the Adult life stage exercise can tell you

Knowing your optimum stage of development, and the tasks characteristic of that stage, can tell you whether you are typical of other adults of a comparable age. If your assessment places you in a category that is different from what other adults of a comparable age are experiencing – ie, you are ahead of or behind others in your development – your discomfort may be the result of having to deal with inappropriate tasks. If your stage of development places you in the appropriate age grouping, your feelings of distress may be caused by a questioning of your life's goals and beliefs, which are characteristic of each development stage. Such information can help you cope with your life-tasks and can help show you what needs to be done to get through that stage.

While each stage is general and reflects averages, differences do appear in our development. The common denominator of the changes we experience is what we face, not how we face it. What this exercise can help you to determine is:

1. Life tasks appropriate to your stage of development

2. What obstacles you need to overcome

3. That your feelings of distress may be 'normal', and that you just need to 'stay with it'.

4. That your feelings of distress are not necessarily caused by your organisation or by some 'wrong' decision you made .

The Stages of Adulthood

The following are features of the different life stages:

Pulling up roots (Ages 16-20)

During this stage we seek independence from home and parents or guardians. We ask 'who are we?', 'what do we want to be, and what do we want to do?' We are interested in 'the world', in the values we have inherited and whether they have meaning for us as we become independent, explore relationships, and test boundaries, feeling our way in a world that is 'new', which we are keen to understand and engage with.

Provisional Adulthood (Ages 20-28)

During this stage, we are 'out' on our own and are making our first commitments to work, stable relationships and family, and other adult responsibilities. During provisional adulthood, we first put to use all of the parental upbringing, education and advice that was part of our childhood and adolescence. Rarely analyzing commitments, it is time to explore the real world of career, relationships and lifestyle.

Age – 30 Transition (Ages 28 – 32)

During this transition stage, initial commitments of our life-style are often re-examined and their meanings questioned. The surface bravado of the provisional period wavers as life begins to look more complex. Many times we will become impatient with the early choices we made and will feel a new vitality springing from within to answer the question 'What do I really want out of life?' Careers and marriages become particularly vulnerable to reassessment. Long-range implications of continuing with current career, community, and life-style are challenged. In many people, change will occur, and in many others, there will be a renewed commitment and reaffirmation of their current career, life style and community. This is often a particularly difficult time for women in our present period of history.

Rooting (Ages 32 – 39)

After going through the age-30 transition, we often tend to get our heads down and get on with life. It is a time when we might seek a mentor – a patron or supporter to show us the ropes. Then at about age 35, the time-squeeze begins. Perhaps it is the first emotional awareness that death will come and that time is running out. We now want more than ever to become established. When we start a career or family, we launch them with certain goals and dreams. Some of these are attainable and desirable and others are not. This time-squeeze during the rooting process often begins to worry us. 'Is there still time to change? '

Midlife Transition (Ages 39 – 45)

This is a period which for many has been labelled as midcareer or midlife crisis. It is often a period of acute personal discomfort in which we may face the gap between youthful dreams and actual fulfilments.

Likely limits of success and achievement become more apparent. There may be a difference between what we have reached and what we want. For some people, this transition is merely a decade milestone. For others, it can be a painful time of crisis. It is a lonely time, because each person is ultimately alone on the journey. Children are growing up and going away, and for many their parents are now looking to them for support. We ask many self-searching questions in this period, such as 'What's in it for me?' 'Where am I having fun?' 'Why can't I be accepted for what I am, not what "they" (spouse, boss, society) expect me to be?' 'Is there one last chance to make it big?' In the search for answers that often consumes the midlife transition period, we may turn to a new career or other new directions in life. We may live out life dramas that we haven't yet finished, or that we refuse to allow to lie down and die.

Restabilization and Flowering (Ages 45 – 55)

Once we have gone through the midlife transition, faced mortality, and forged a new life-style, this stage can feel like the best time of life. Often unrushed by the sense of urgency of the thirties, a new stability can be achieved. A career often takes a sharp turn upward. Money becomes less important. Life can become more stable because we listen more to the inner voice than to external demands. We may experience increasing attention to a few old values and a few friends. One hypothesis is that in this and the next stage, if we lose a spouse or close friend, we may go back into provisional-adulthood patterns, trying out life options all over again.

Mellowing and Renewal (Ages 55 – 65+)

At this stage, people tend to become more satisfied with themselves, coming to grips with what they have and haven't done. At first, there is little concern with either past or future, but eventually questions arise as to when to retire, what to do, and how to cope with sudden changes in life-style. It is a difficult step because nearly all of our life is attuned to paid work. Thus an abrupt shift to leisure is sometimes traumatic. The impact of this decision can be compounded by ageing, termination of long-time associations and friendships, and frequently by a total lack of preparation.

Watch Point

Be wary of 'stage theories' that tell you what you should be doing, thinking or Feeling at any time. Life is not as neat as that. We can be largely restabilising and flowering but also be dealing with some leftover mid-life transition issues, or even some rooting.

The value of research like this is not to create new psychological and behavioural strait jackets for us, but to let us know that the changes and complexity we might be experiencing are not being experienced in isolation. But although the process is valid enough in general there will be considerable individual differences.

Likewise, the process described now belongs to this historical epoch. It would be rash to presume that fifty years from now, within a different society with likely new concepts of work, leisure, and the family, that the stages would be as they are described here.

Gail Sheehy in her book, *Pathfinders*, did a nationwide (USA) survey of reported satisfaction from men and women which produced some fascinating differences. The table on page 78 summarises her findings.

From a careful examination of this table it is clear that the many conflicting pressures on contemporary women summed up by the dilemma employment vs. child rearing, are reflected by her findings that from their late 20 s women get increasingly dissatisfied with life and only catch up again with men in their early 50 s. Her research also suggests that women take longer to resolve their mid-life transitions than men, causing an uncomfortable diamond shape between 40-55 on the figure. This represents a period when the sexes are furthest apart in terms of life satisfactions.

Women only really became happier than men at the end of their lives, (presumably after many of the men have died!) The pressures on marriages in mid-life are summarised in the table on page 79.

THE HAPPIEST YEARS

A Comparison Between Men and Women

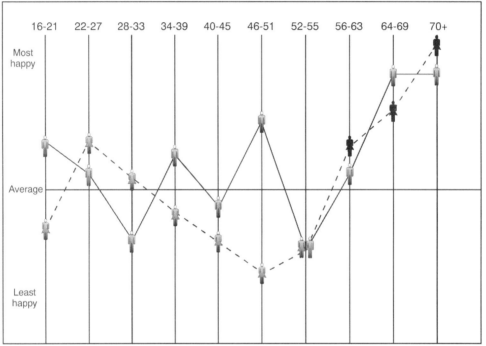

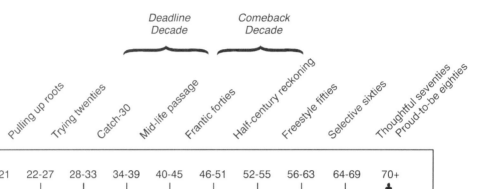

			Deadline Decade		Comeback Decade				
Pulling up roots	Trying twenties	Catch-30	Mid-life passage	Frantic forties	Half-century reckoning	Freestyle fifties	Selective sixties	Thoughtful seventies	Proud-to-be eighties
16-21	22-27	28-33	34-39	40-45	46-51	52-55	56-63	64-69	70+

Reproduced with permission from Gail Sheehy, *Pathfinders*, Sidgwick & Jackson

Marcel Proust in his book 'Remembrance of Things Past' noted that everyone of us:

'is a creature without any fixed age who has... the faculty of becoming, in a few seconds, many years younger, and who, surrounded by the walls of the time through which he has lived, floats within them but as though in a basin the surface level of which is constantly changing, so as to bring him into the range now of one epoch, now of another.'

Daniel Levinson, expanding on this theme, says that:

'only after we understand the profound significance of the epochs in our lives... can we understand the ways in which one is, at a single time, a child, a youth, a middle-aged and an elderly person. We are never ageless. As we gain a greater sense of our own biographies, however, we can begin to exist at multiple ages. In the process we do not fragment ourselves, rather we become more integrated and whole.'

One Common Form of Marriage Crisis At Mid-Life

	WIFE	**HUSBAND**
Age		
25-35	Vicariously enjoys husband's career and its rewards, while providing support. Suppresses feelings and:	Suppresses feelings and focuses energy on career achievement.

GIVES ▼	**GETS** ▲
Emotional, Housekeeping, Maternal, and Sexual Support	Money Status Security Children

	WIFE	**HUSBAND**
35-40	Children grow up. She decides vicarious rewards aren't really worth it and begins to feel 'used'. She withdraws support and puts energy into personal growth and achievement for herself. She begins to discover ambition.	He has either accomplished all his goals or discovers he can't; in either case he ends up saying, 'Is there nothing more?' His suppressed feelings explode. His need for support sky-rockets. He begins to re-discover feelings.
40-45	Leads her to think: 'Why can't he pull himself together like a good husband so I can go out and develop myself without feeling guilty?'	Leads him to think: 'What the hell is she doing running off in other directions while I'm falling apart?'

Leading to....

Explosion in the marriage

Keep a record

- Your scores from the life stage questionnaire
- Notes about how your findings from the questionnaire compared with your actual age and feelings

A Gallery of Life Stage Problems

Do I recognise myself?

In the illustration below are five pictures which represent some of the most common life-stage problems we encounter when working with people in organisations.

The important thing to remember is that all of these problems are normal.

A GALLERY OF LIFE-STAGE PROBLEMS

SALLY SECRETARY
34 years old

'I do seem to have as many skills as a lot of my so-called bosses.'

'My boss keeps pushing me to become more ambitious.'

'Is it worth it when I would have to move if and when my husband moves?'

'I really could do an administrative/ supervisory job – couldn't I?'

'My husband wouldn't mind as long as it doesn't affect him or the children.'

PETER PLATEAU
45 years old

'Why doesn't my boss give me challenging asignments?'

'Why am I always being passed over?'

'Why do my children seem to believe in everything I don't?'

'Just what do you have to do to get promoted around here?'

'Why can't my wife and I communicate?'

If you see yourself amongst these descriptions, this does not mean that your own uniqueness is in any way reduced, but it might help to see yourself in perspective. All of these people are desperately in need of RAINBOWS. By working through this book they could all create opportunities for themselves to build some.

CATHY CATCHTHIRTY
30 years old

'I really would like a baby – wouldn't I?'

'Why can't I be satisfied with what I've got? Most women in my situation would be happy.'

'I know I'm doing well, but something seems missing.'

'Why am I so depressed?'

'I don't really want a baby – do I?'

TOM TECHNICIAN
26 years old

'This really seems as far as I can go with my qualifications.'

'If I do all that studying it will really take up a lot of my social life and domestic time. Will it all be worth it?'

'Do I want to be an engineer with all that would be involved?'

'Can I be certain that there will be a good job for me at the end of it all?'

MICHAEL MELLOWED
53 years old

'What else can I do at my age?'

'Perhaps I should give someone else a chance.'

'Can I really spend another 12 years just doing the same thing?'

'I've spent a good part of my life doing this. I've done it well, and I've done well – but there's no challenge any more. It's all too easy.'

'Could I afford to make a change? My kids have left home, but my wife is used to a good standard of living.'

Rainbow Building Progress Check

WHERE AM I NOW?

What did you learn from the adult life stage questionnaire?

What have you learned about your 'life stage problems'?
Do you have any?

....
....
....
....
....
....
....
....
....
....
....
....
....
....
....
....
....
....

Your Career Pattern

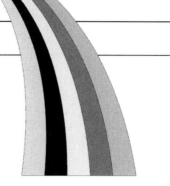

Just as the concept of WORK is changing dramatically, so and not surprisingly, is our concept of CAREER.

Traditionally the word career has come to mean a succession of jobs each of which has higher status than its predecessor with a progressively rising income. This usage became so current that people who did not progress in this way were sometimes referred to as merely having 'jobs', while those who did progress had 'careers'.

We can now recognise that it makes more sense to distinguish between a variety of CAREER PATTERNS.

Following the work in the United States of Michael Driver, we would distinguish between four major career patterns from which people tend to choose. The diagram overleaf describes the four patterns, states at what life stages this choice tends to be made, the frequency of occupational changes that the people – given the choice – would make, and the directions of the career pattern viewed in hierarchical terms. It also summarises the motives behind the choice of pattern.

These people are examples of the different patterns:

HORIZONTAL

John (40 years old)
'I've never had a job for more than two years. I get bored. I don't always leave for more money. Sometimes I've earned less. But I like learning new things, meeting new people – it's interesting. I don't suppose I'll ever change now. Some people think my jobs are 'dead-end jobs', but I reckon some of those folks who spend all their lives working their way up are half-dead by the time they get there.'

STEADY

Carol (30 years old)
'I've always wanted to be a nurse. Even before I went to school I had a nurse's uniform. It would be nice to get to be a sister but I'm not really bothered. I'd hate to be a matron – all that book work and responsibility, and you don't have the same relationships with your patients. I'll do this until they kick me out.'

VERTICAL

Charles (55 years old)
'I always wanted a good job with prospects. I've always been ambitious, and I've done well. I had to swap firms a bit during my 30's and 40's but each one moved me up a rung or two. I like the responsibility now. I like making decisions.'

CYCLICAL

Janette (49 years old)
'I really like to get involved in what I'm doing, but I do like learning new things. I made a vow to myself in my 20s that no matter how well I was doing, every 5 five years or so I'd take a good hard look and see if it was still exciting

me. If not, I change. I've changed occupations three times now and don't regret one of them. I hope to do at least two more very different jobs before I die.'

Exercise 15: Which career pattern do I want?*

Look at the table on the next page and then answer these questions.

> Which career pattern is the closest to the one I've had?

Circle your choice:

HORIZONTAL

STEADY

VERTICAL

CYCLICAL

> Which is the closest to the one I would like in the future?

Circle your choice.

HORIZONTAL

STEADY

VERTICAL

CYCLICAL

CAREER PATTERNS				
	HORIZONTAL: 'VARIETY'	STEADY: 'MORE OF THE SAME'	VERTICAL: 'THE LADDER'	CYCLICAL: 'THE 5-YEAR ITCH'
WHEN CHOICE OF PATTERN IS MADE	Never. People do not consciously 'make a choice'	Teenage choice	Teenage choice	Every 5-10 years
HOW OFTEN OCCUPATIONS ARE CHANGED	1-2 years	Never or rarely unless forced	Never or rarely unless forced. Jobs are changed for advancement	5-10 years
HOW OFTEN OCCUPATIONS ARE CHANGED	Levels are not relevant	Stays the same	Upwards	Levels are not relevant
MOTIVE FOR CHOOSING THIS PATTERN	Variety, challenge, 'doing what you want to do, regardless	Security, intrinsic job satisfaction, wanting a 'job for life'	Achievement, status, material success, power	Variety, personal growth

There are many decisions to be made about career patterns before making a final selection. We will come back to this later.

DECISION 1. Do I want to work full-time or part-time?

Part-time work is increasing rapidly. It has been affected less than full-time employment by recession and the shift from an Industrial to a Post-Industrial Economy.

What we are really seeing is a change in our concept of employment. People are beginning to ask themselves for how many hours they wish to perform paid work each week, or even, in a year. The average working week is reducing, albeit slowly, so that we can anticipate a future where people have a real choice about the number of hours they work. These might range from a few hours a week to 50 hours or more a week, spread over a few weeks a year at one extreme, or nearly every week at the other.

Even now it is possible to achieve a level of flexibility in terms of working hours that was unthinkable a few years ago.

DECISION 2. Will I be employed by someone else or will I work for myself?

The fastest growing area of the economy is self-employment. There has been almost a 30% increase in the past ten years. The enormous growth of the 'black economy' also demonstrates how many people like to work for themselves.

The majority of new jobs are being created in small businesses. We can no longer look to large companies to provide the nation with new jobs. To expand and develop, they have to shed labour, not increase it. As a result an increasing number of people are moving towards small business start-up and self-employment. However, it is a fact that the great majority of new businesses fail within the first few years of operation. You should take great care before embarking on this route.

The following exercise will help you come to a decision as to whether self-employment would suit you.

Exercise 16: Am I suited to self-employment?

- The table opposite sets out some arguments for and against self-employment. Put a tick in the box if you are attracted by what it says, a cross if you don't like the idea.

- If you scored 11 to 15 ticks in 'A', then you are clearly the type to be attracted by the idea of working on your own account. If you scored between 8 and 10, you are drawn to the idea, but should find out more about it. If you scored 7 ticks or less, you are the cautious type.

- On 'B', if you have 11 to 15 ticks, you are prepared to go on with the idea, even though you see how difficult it could be. If you scored between 6 and 10 ticks, you are interested, but still anxious. If you ticked 5 or less, and put a lot of crosses, you'd better off in a regular job.

- What was your overall score, adding the total for 'A' to the total for 'B'? If you scored 20 ticks out of a possible 30, self-employment could well be the route for you. If you try these tests again in a year's time, you could score very differently.

PRO's & CON's OF SELF-EMPLOYMENT

A By being self-employed...

☐	1	I would be my own boss
☐	2	I could work when I wanted to and stop when I felt like it
☐	3	I could use my own money to do something useful
☐	4	I would be free and independent
☐	5	I would learn about business
☐	6	I would improve my self-confidence
☐	7	I would be able to work day and night at something I like doing
☐	8	I would avoid being unemployed and all the problems that go with it
☐	9	I would welcome the chance to think up an idea for a business
☐	10	I would have to make plans
☐	11	I would have to organise my time carefully
☐	12	I would be able to make money out of an idea I've got
☐	13	I could make a lot of money
☐	14	It would give me experiences which I could use later in life
☐	15	I could look for other jobs while working as a self-employed person

☐ **How many ticks did you score out of 15?**

B By being self-employed...

☐	1	I would have to work on my own a lot
☐	2	I might have to spend all my savings
☐	3	I would have to start work early every morning
☐	4	I would probably have to work in the evenings
☐	5	I would have to organise myself and my work very carefully
☐	6	I would have to persuade other people to help me
☐	7	I would have to sell things or ideas to strangers
☐	8	I would have to find premises or run the business away from home
☐	9	I would have to give up a wage or a benefit which I could receive each week
☐	10	I may have to borrow money from the family or the bank
☐	11	I may have to give up a regular job
☐	12	I may have to go to evening class to learn business skills
☐	13	I would have to find out if there's any need or demand for my skill or product
☐	14	I would have to find out how to keep business records
☐	15	I would have to work very hard

☐ **How many ticks did you score out of 15?**

Adapted with permission from Your Own Business, Hobson's Press, 1983.

Decision 3. Am I or will I be part of a dual career family?

We believe strongly in the value of a couple doing this programme together. This actually becomes essential if both partners have jobs. Couples are beginning to discover that having a dual-career family can offer greater opportunities for each individual than if either was the sole breadwinner. It makes sense to decide what income is required as a family and then examine the various alternatives. This can then enable both partners to share more in parenting if they wish or to develop other interests and unpaid work skills that possessing a full-time job would inhibit.

Real life examples have included:

- Both partners taking part-time jobs

- One partner taking a year off to do other things

- One partner decreasing his/her job to 75% to provide time for other activities.

The figure below shows a wide spectrum of career relationships possible within the context of a marriage.

> Where on the spectrum am I and my partner?

This figure makes it clear that we should not always take for granted what people mean when they say that they are a 'dual-career family'. The majority of such couples may have dual careers but they may not have an egalitarian relationship when it comes to domestic responsibilities.

Exercise 17: Pros and cons of a dual career family

- Each partner makes a list of:

  A The advantages of being part of a dual career family
  B The disadvantages of being part of a dual career family.

- The lists are shared and discussed, and the following questions asked:

> Overall, do we wish to be a dual career family?
>
> What are the implications for us of being a dual career family?

A SPECTRUM OF RELATIONSHIPS FOR COUPLES

THE TRADITIONAL COUPLE	THE SEMI-TRADITIONAL COUPLE	THE TYPICAL DUAL-CAREER COUPLE	THE EGALITARIAN COUPLE
HE is the breadwinner. SHE is the homemaker and child-raiser.	HE is the breadwinner (with some involvement in family and home). SHE is the homemaker and child-raiser but she also works, usually for a specific purpose (such as better vacations for the family, extra home comforts, her own personal satisfaction.)	HE is committed to a professional career. SHE is committed to a professional career.	HIS and HER roles vis-à-vis career and home are essentially the same.
HE competes and succeeds for both. SHE provides child care, and social maintenance for both.	HE has the dominant career but acknowledges her contribution to their quality of life, and her need for some kind of outside activity. SHE works, but neither of them thinks of her as having a 'career'.	The couple think of themselves as being a dual-career family. BUT, one of them (almost always the woman) takes on more than 50 per cent of the responsibility for housekeeping and child-raising, and provides less than 50 per cent of the income.	BOTH work; they have an equal commitment to their jobs. BOTH do 50 per cent of the housework. BOTH do 50 per cent of the child-raising.

Note: Couples often change their relationships on the spectrum. Perhaps the most typical example we see of this today is the couple who in their twenties assume a traditional couple role. In their thirties, after their children are in school, they shift to the semi-traditional role. And in their forties, after the children have left home, they become a dual career couple. In practice, however, at this stage women typically may be a number of years behind men who have held full-time unintgerrupted careers.

DECISION 4. What career pattern do I want?

You are now ready to focus again on the underlying career pattern required, as discussed on page 83, and to make your decision.

This completes the basic process represented in the diagram below.

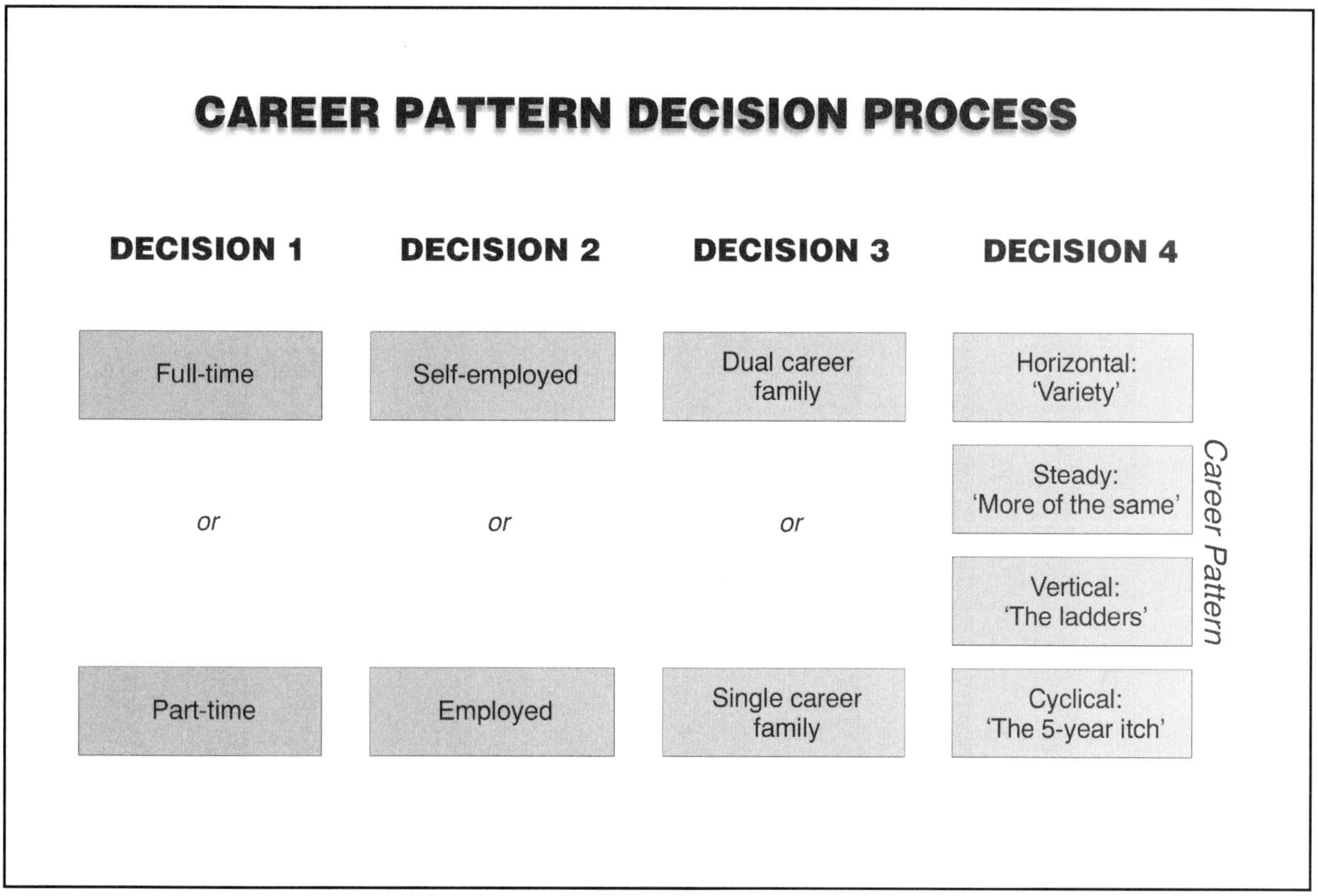

Keep a record

• My notes and options
• Career patterns which I might Consider

CAREER PATTERN DECISION PROCESS

DECISION 1	DECISION 2	DECISION 3	DECISION 4
Full-time	Self-employed	Dual career family	Horizontal: 'Variety'
			Steady: 'More of the same'
or	*or*	*or*	Vertical: 'The ladders'
Part-time	Employed	Single career family	Cyclical: 'The 5-year itch'

Career Pattern

Rainbow Building Progress Check

WHERE AM I?

What have you learned about the possibilities for your own career pattern?

....
....
....
....
....
....
....
....
....
....
....
....
....
....
....
....

Up until now, you have been involved primarily in collecting data from yourself only, on who and where you are. The final section of Question 2 will involve you in getting data from other important people in your life.

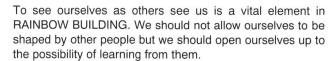

Who are you? What do others think?

To see ourselves as others see us is a vital element in RAINBOW BUILDING. We should not allow ourselves to be shaped by other people but we should open ourselves up to the possibility of learning from them.

A useful way of looking at oneself is through a window† which demonstrates the different facets that contribute to that unique individual – ME!

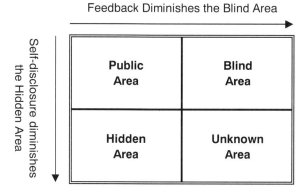

Feedback Diminishes the Blind Area

Self-disclosure diminishes the Hidden Area

| Public Area | Blind Area |
| Hidden Area | Unknown Area |

PUBLIC AREA: This refers to those aspects of ourselves that we know about and that we are comfortable for others to know about too.

BLIND AREA: Those parts of ourselves that others see but of which we remain in blissful ignorance. This has been called the 'bad breath area', but this only refers to negative aspects of ourselves. Often we are unaware of positive or interesting things that people think and feel about us because they have never told us and we have never asked them.

HIDDEN AREA: Our innermost thoughts and feelings, expressed to few or perhaps to no one.

UNKNOWN AREA: This is sometimes called the area of potential growth. It refers to the potential we all possess that has not yet come to light.

Only by getting feedback from others can we discover more of the blind and unknown areas of ourselves.

Exercise 17: How do others see you?*

RAINBOW BUILDING SKILL: *Knowing yourself*
Research skills
Communicating

This exercise involves a process that you might wish to initiate to a greater or lesser extent.

You should have completed exercises on the following:

1. My lifeline
2. How do I spend my time?
3. My work and play values
4. Finding my transferable skills
5. What are my interests?
6. Choosing where to live
7. The ages of me
8. What lite stage am I at now?
9. What kind of career pattern do I want?

You will undoubtedly obtain value from talking through your answers to these, and any of the other exercises, with friends and colleagues, but there are particular exercises where additional data can be invaluable. Here are some suggestions that have been carried out by participants on our workshops:

• Get a spouse, partner or close friend to do the WORK VALUES card sort in terms of the values they see you demonstrating. From this you will learn which values they see you expressing as well as merely holding.

• Ask friends and colleagues to do the TRANSFERABLE SKILLS card sort according to how they see your skills.

• Ask colleagues and your bosses what skills they see you as owning. Ask them also what areas for development they see in you.

• Ask a spouse, partner or friend to do the INTERESTS check according to what interests they see you as having.

• In addition to these you might like to ask your spouse or partner to do the exercises on where *they* would like to live and work.

†This model was developed by Joe Luft and Harry Ingrams and is commonly called the JO-HARI WINDOW.

Rainbow Building Summary Sheet

WHERE AM I NOW?

I am at the following LIFE-STAGE:	The career pattern I want: (circle)			
....	HORIZONTAL	STEADY	VERTICAL	CYCLICAL
....	FULL-TIME		PART-TIME	
....	SELF-EMPLOYED		EMPLOYED	
....	DUAL CAREER FAMILY		SINGLE CAREER FAMILY	

I have learned the following about myself from other people:

....

....

....

....

....

On the basis of that I will:

....

....

....

....

....

You are now about midway through this career and life management programme. You have collected a great deal of data about yourself from yourself and from others. Reflect on the following and record your thoughts for your AHA! Folder.

How do I feel about myself and who and where I am right now?

What changes would I like to make?

Reviewing Your Contract

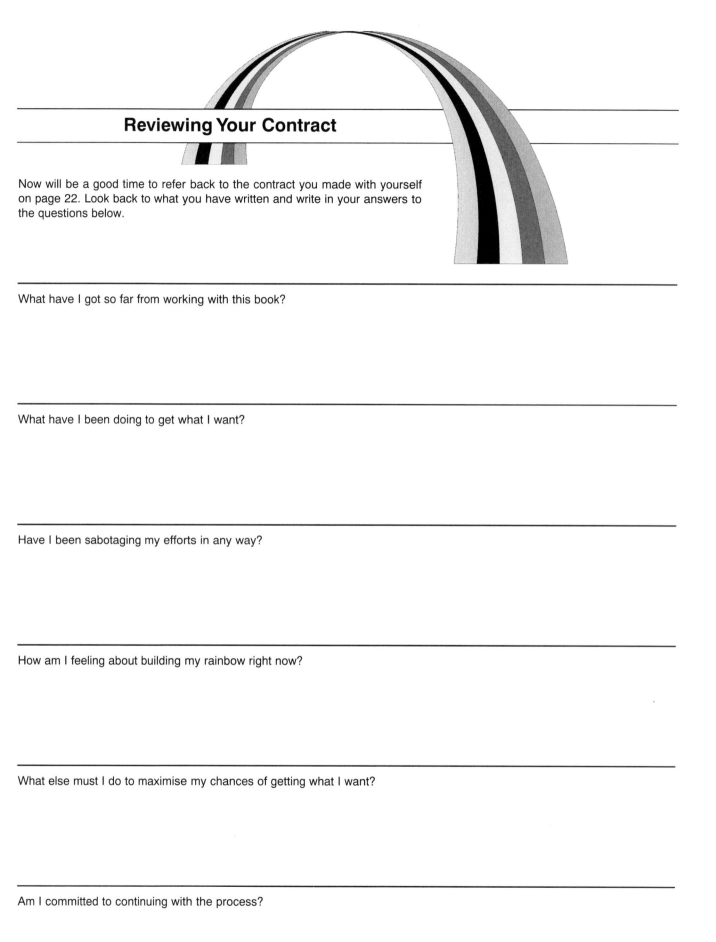

Now will be a good time to refer back to the contract you made with yourself on page 22. Look back to what you have written and write in your answers to the questions below.

What have I got so far from working with this book?

What have I been doing to get what I want?

Have I been sabotaging my efforts in any way?

How am I feeling about building my rainbow right now?

What else must I do to maximise my chances of getting what I want?

Am I committed to continuing with the process?

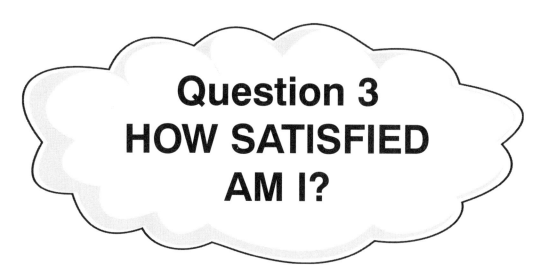

Question 3
HOW SATISFIED AM I?

Having thought about 'who you are' in terms of your career and life so far, the next step is to reflect on the amount of satisfaction and dissatisfaction you are currently experiencing. Satisfactions can be clues to what is important to you and what you may want to preserve and retain. Dissatisfactions, on the other hand, are clues to what in your career or life may need remedying. This is not to say that you can achieve everything you desire, which is clearly not the case, as constraints – both internal and external – must limit everybody's range of choice. Frequently, however, we limit our thinking by focusing so directly on the constraints operating on us that we are able to achieve less than we might. In consequence, our careers or lives may not be as consciously shaped, chosen or satisfying as they might be.

The exercises in this section will help you to focus in turn on:

• your sources of satisfaction

• what you would like more, or less of in either your present job, your career or your life

• objectives you may wish to set in order to achieve more of what you feel is important to you.

ROUTE MAP
for "How Satisfied Am I?"

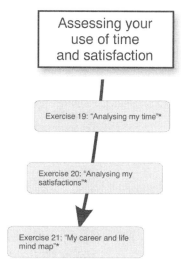

Assessing your use of time and satisfaction

Exercise 19: "Analysing my time"*

Exercise 20: "Analysing my satisfactions"*

Exercise 21: "My career and life mind map"*

Assessing Your Use of Time and Satisfactions

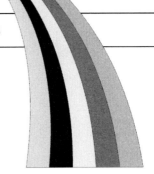

On page 25, you have already completed your TIME INVESTMENT RECORD and asked yourself questions about this. It is now time to begin to assess the level of satisfaction you are getting from that investment when compared with the time spent.

We find it useful to distinguish between MAINTENANCE, SOLD and DISCRETIONARY time.

• MAINTENANCE TIME

This is the amount of time spent maintaining yourself or others, cleaning, eating, tidying, shopping, cooking etc. Keeping things ticking over in your life.

• SOLD TIME

This is the time you 'sell' to an employer, an organisation or a customer, to produce income or some other reward. This concept is wider than simply the hours you spend 'doing' your job. It involves travelling-to-work time, follow-up time, etc.

• DISCRETIONARY TIME

This is the time you have free to choose exactly how you want to spend it. This may not always mean that you will enjoy what you choose to do. You may feel a responsibility to attend a local committee meeting, visit relatives, spend time learning about car maintenance because you cannot afford to pay for servicing, and you might not particularly enjoy any of them. It is your choice, however. It may not always feel like you have a choice, but you do.

THERE IS ALWAYS AN ALTERNATIVE

You may choose not to live with the consequences of an alternative, for example, being considered by your community as non-community minded, or facing criticism or your own guilt feelings for not visiting your relatives. But for every situation there are alternatives.

Sometimes the distinctions between these three elements of our time can be difficult to make. Everyday cooking is clearly a maintenance activity. If it is also a hobby of yours, you may spend much longer at it than you need to. In that case you are devoting some of your discretionary time to cooking too. These distinctions have to be subjective. Only you can decide under which of the three labels a particular activity comes.

Data needed

• Time Investment Record from Exercise 2

Analysing your time

• Refer back to the Time Investment Record you made in Exercise 2.

• Use 3 differently coloured pencils/pens to colour in each section according to whether it is maintenance, sold or discretionary time.

• Now work through the Time Investment Record and make lists of your activities in each of the three categories using labels that make sense to you. Your lists might look something like the ones below:

Maintenance Time	Sold Time	Discretionary Time
• Sleeping	• At work	• Time with my
• Eating	• Travelling to work	spouse/partner
• Cleaning	• Taking work home at weekends	• Walking, etc.

• Take a large sheet of paper. Write your lists down the left hand side and mark off in hours, a scale across the top to make a chart like the one shown opposite. The divisions represent hours of time (you should try to get as many as possible across your sheet because 'sleeping' and 'at work' could take up to 60 of them!).

• Looking back at your Time Investment Record add up, as accurately as possible, the total time spent on each activity over the whole week. Mark off the bars on the chart to show the total using the same colours as before. When you have finished check how much of the bars you have coloured in – it should represent about 168 hours (the hours available to you in 1 week).

An example follows.

ANALYSING YOUR TIME – example

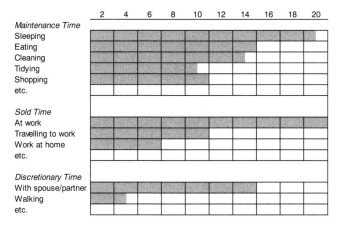

	2	4	6	8	10	12	14	16	18	20
Maintenance Time										
Sleeping										
Eating										
Cleaning										
Tidying										
Shopping										
etc.										
Sold Time										
At work										
Travelling to work										
Work at home										
etc.										
Discretionary Time										
With spouse/partner										
Walking										
etc.										

> **Watch Point**
>
> Beware of too broad categories. In the example above, 'At work' would need to be broken down further and similarly 'Time spent with my spouse/partner' needs to be broken down into doing what and for how long.

Exercise 20: Analysing my satisfactions*

RAINBOW BUILDING SKILL: **Learning from experience**
Knowing yourself

- Work down your list again and make an assessment of how much satisfaction each activity gives you using the star system below.

★	not at all satisfying
★★	
★★★	
★★★★	
★★★★★	extremely satisfying

- Write in your star rating next to each activity on the chart.

> How does your chart look?
> Are your highly rated activities the ones you are spending plenty of time on?
> Are there any shocks?

Making changes

- It's worth thinking about which of the activities you might like to do more of. Not all activities which are relatively satisfying give more satisfaction if you do a lot more of them – they may be better in small but regular doses.

- Look at each of the activities to which you have given a 4 or 5-star rating. Think about which ones really would give you extra satisfaction if you could do more of them. Some will be easier to increase than others.

- If you do want to do more of some activities, where will you find the time? You will have to reduce the time spent on some other activities. Which ones will you choose and how will you spread the cut-backs? Not all activities with a low star rating will be easy to cut, but start by looking at low-rated activities in your 'Discretionary' group...

> Are there any activities which are missing altogether from your busy life that you would like to include?

Other changes to think about

- Look back at your notes about the balance of your life roles (Exercise 2) and see if they suggest any other changes you might want to make.

> Were any of the roles missing from your life?
>
> Do you want to change the balance of time spent in different roles?

Planning an ideal (but realistic) timetable

- You may have decided you would like to increase or decrease the amounts of time spent on some activities, or you may have decided that increases are not necessary but that protection of certain time is. Start with types of activity you wish to increase or protect and make a set of decision statements like the one below.

'I plan to spend at least _____ hours per week doing _____.'

> **Keep a record**
>
> - Your bar charts for time and satisfaction
> - Your ideal chart

Exercise 21: My career and life mind map*

RAINBOW BUILDING SKILL: Knowing yourself

This exercise is designed to take a snapshot of your entire life as you experience it now. This will help you to draw up a list of your primary satisfactions and dissatisfactions. Some of you might prefer to do just that, but we wish to introduce you to a technique that many people find helpful in getting many related and unrelated thoughts onto paper in a short period of time. The technique is called mind mapping and was developed by Tony Buzan, initially to take notes when listening to lectures. The example below may initially look totally chaotic, but closer inspection will reveal the thinking 'flows' that occurred when the person produced this mind map.

The advantages of mind maps over ordinary list-making are that:

- the main idea is more clearly defined;
- the relative importance of each idea is clearly indicated, as more important ideas will be nearer the centre and less important nearer the edge;
- new information is easily added;
- the links between ideas are easier to see.

The example below will give you an idea of the process.

You always begin a mind map in the centre of a large piece of paper with the key concept, in this case 'My life and my career'. See what comes into your head. Branch out from the centre. Name the branch lines close to the centre (such as Present, Home, etc. in the example given). Take the exercise as far as your mind wants to take it.

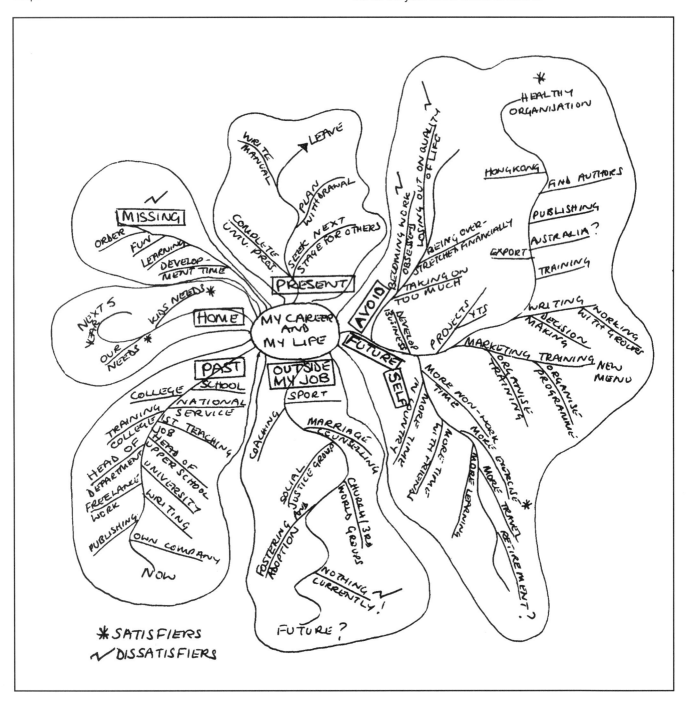

Print your words in capitals; the pattern will be easier to read later.

The printed words should be on lines and each line connected to other lines.

Do not worry about order or presentation as this will interrupt your thinking flow. In many cases you will find that this will take care of itself. Put everything you can think of around the central idea.

After you have finished, see what links to what and connect them up.

You can always draw the map again if it will make it easier to understand .

Use different colours to distinguish between your primary branches, either by writing with different colours or by circling the branches with different colours.

Colours, shapes, symbols, arrows, etc, can be used.

- Use one colour to refer to conditions, aspects, ideas, etc, in your mind map that will denote 'satisfiers'. Circle any item that seems to be a 'satisfier' for you.

  List all your satisfiers on a separate sheet of paper. Each time one is mentioned, write it down, eg,

family

job

friends

travel

community activities

learning/studying

- On the same sheet of paper write down the answers to the following questions by drawing the appropriate words from your list:

> Who are the key people in my life and career?
> What do I need from my paid and unpaid work?
> What do I enjoy doing?
> What surprised me in my list?

> Is there anything missing? Would I have expected some satisfiers to be here which are not? Why aren't they on my brain pattern? Which of my satisfiers would I like more of?

- Now circle all the items on your mind map that are 'dissatisfiers' in some way. Use another colour for this. You might even find that some items classify both as satisfiers and dissatisfiers.

- List all your dissatisfiers on a separate sheet of paper as you did for the list of satisfiers.

- Write down your answers to the following questions:

> Who are the key people in my dissatisfiers?
> What do I need from my paid and unpaid work?
> What don't I enjoy doing?

> What surprised me in my list?
>
> Is there anything missing?
>
> Which of my dissatisfiers do I want to do something about?

Keep a record

- Your mind map
- Lists of satisfiers and dissatisfiers

Rainbow Building Summary Sheet

HOW SATISFIED AM I?

You have analysed in greater depth just what pay-offs you are getting from how you spend your time. You have delved into what really gives you satisfaction in your career and your life and explored the causes of your dissatisfaction. Participants on our workshops have found it useful to summarise these under the headings of People and Activities. However, if you have items that do not really fit this classification, ignore the classification. It is only an aid, and as with all the aids in this book, if it does not work for you – don't use it!

My major SATISFIERS are:

	People	Activities
IN MY JOB		
IN MY CAREER		
IN MY LIFE		

My major DISSATISFIERS are:

	People	Activities
IN MY JOB		
IN MY CAREER		
IN MY LIFE		

Question 4
WHAT CHANGES DO I WANT?

It is not our claim that everybody can attain or achieve absolutely everything – we do believe, however, that most of us rarely achieve much that we are capable of, largely because we do not become clear about what we want or would prefer to be doing. Until we do, we cannot even begin the journey towards our next stage of development through which we will realise more of our potential and achieve more of what is important to us.

ROUTE MAP

for "What Changes Do I Want?"

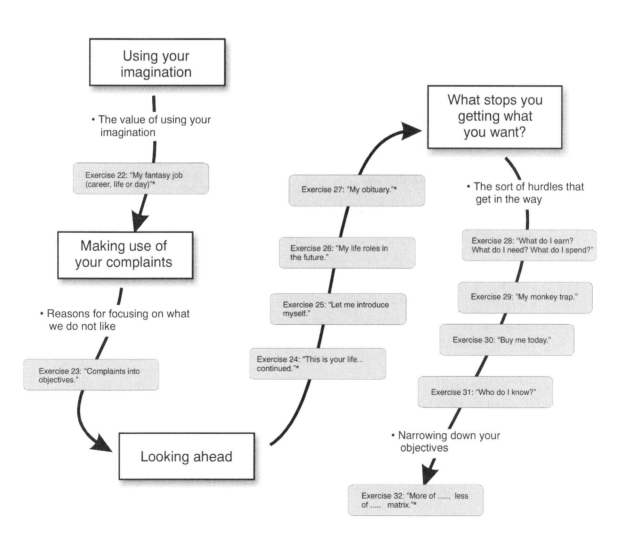

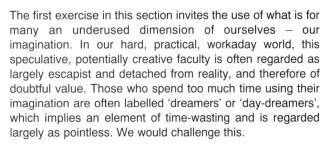

Using Your Imagination

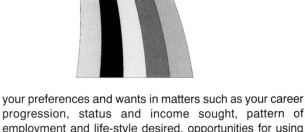

The first exercise in this section invites the use of what is for many an underused dimension of ourselves – our imagination. In our hard, practical, workaday world, this speculative, potentially creative faculty is often regarded as largely escapist and detached from reality, and therefore of doubtful value. Those who spend too much time using their imagination are often labelled 'dreamers' or 'day-dreamers', which implies an element of time-wasting and is regarded largely as pointless. We would challenge this.

In using your imagination, or in a fantasy journey, what you can do is to get in touch with those possibilities which would be interesting, attractive or desirable for you. Such flights of fancy can provide clues as to where you would like to be, or what you might want to work towards – which, because it seems too impractical, you may have scarcely even bothered to think about. Using your imagination, thinking the unthinkable, dreaming the impossible, need not be a waste of time.

This kind of exercise will be easier for some personality styles than for others. The practical, logical person might respond less enthusiastically, inclining towards hard, researched, proven data and methods. The enthusiastic individual often takes more readily to the possibility. Whatever your inclination, however, we would suggest there are gains to be made from an excursion into the realm of fantasy. Have a go!

**Exercise 22: My fantasy job
(career, life or day)***

- You are to imagine for a time that there are no constraints for you of time, money, age, health, status, ties etc. This exercise asks you to remove all thoughts of constraints for the next few minutes – ignore them!

- Appreciating that there are no restrictions, select one of the following to work on. Begin with which ever seems easiest and put a ring around it:

  MY FANTASY JOB

  MY FANTASY CAREER

  MY FANTASY DAY

  MY FANTASY LIFE

- Think through your chosen topic in some detail and write down your version of what would be involved eg, in your FANTASY JOB, identify details such as status, salary, job specification, style of work, the life-style which accompanies it, what you would actually do and not do, with whom you would work, in what kind of surroundings, with what kind of authority and responsibilities, with what kind of working day, week etc.

In your FANTASY CAREER, go into the area of your career as a whole, commenting, for example, on how it might ideally develop from your present position. Include

your preferences and wants in matters such as your career progression, status and income sought, pattern of employment and life-style desired, opportunities for using your present skills and developing others, integration of your career development with other life-roles or opportunities you hope will occur for you etc.

Your FANTASY DAY is an invitation to log the events of what for you would be the 'perfect day'. Where would you be, what would you do, and with whom, if anybody? What time would the day start and end, would it include work, leisure, family and in what proportion etc?

Your FANTASY LIFE offers an opportunity to consider your ideal life as a whole. In this fantasy, you can outline what would be your scenario for the perfect life. This picture could include how long you would like to live, the pattern of work, the integration of work, home and social life, status, income, life-style etc.

In short, whichever topic you choose, write in as much detail as you can so that the fantasy becomes a full picture rather than simply an outline. (Some people prefer to represent the details of their fantasy in picture form or through symbols rather than in written words – if you prefer to do it that way, please do. The fact remains that the more details you have, the more use the exercise is likely to be to you.).

- When you have written down your FANTASY, it is ready to be worked on. Think carefully through the following:

> What are my thoughts, feelings and reactions to doing the exercise?
>
> What does the fantasy indicate about what I would value, appreciate, aspire to or want for myself?

> What are the differences between my fantasy and my reality?
>
> How much of my fantasy is achievable at present or might be in the future? If I can't have it all, can I have some of it?

What are the barriers to my achieving some of my fantasy and how might these be overcome?

What would be the consequences of my working to achieve some of the features of my fantasy, for myself and other people?

Would the pursuit of the features of my fantasy and their achievements be worth the possible consequences?

What objectives would I like to set myself on the basis of this exercise?

'The danger of premature evaluation is that nothing will be conceived'
Roger von Oech

You see things as they are: and you ask 'Why?'
But I dream things that never were: and I ask 'Why not?'
G B Shaw

Make a note of any objectives you have identified and place these in your AHA! Folder.

Keep a record

• Your fantasy

• Things you would need to change to achieve your fantasy

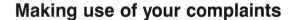

Making use of your complaints

Exercise 23: Complaints into objectives

Sometimes it is easier for us to focus on what we do not like in a particular situation than on what we do like. Irritants and dissatisfactions are often easy to identify because of the discomfort they cause – it is difficult to ignore things which actually hurt. But remember, pain has the purpose of alerting us to something which needs attention.

Our complaints and dissatisfactions can therefore be used positively. They bring to our notice something we would prefer to be different and they form the starting points from which to make changes – so that things will be more like we want them to be.

By being explicit about what we don't like, we can discover more of what we do like. Complaints can be converted into objectives !

This exercise invites you to look at current complaints you may have about your job, career or life and to use them to begin to identify what you might work to change.

- CLARIFYING COMPLAINTS. Sometimes dissatisfactions are expressed in very general terms, eg, I am not getting much out of my job at the moment – and this means they are difficult to translate into objectives. To help make your complaints specific, the exercise asks you to look at your job in more detail. If you choose to look at your life, your career, or just one day, you will probably need to add your own categories of sources of dissatisfaction.

But, just for this example, our focus is on features of our *job* which commonly provide sources of dissatisfaction – if for you there are other sources, then simply add them to the left-hand column.

In the 'COMPLAINTS' column of the chart note quite briefly any significant complaint you may have in a particular area – consider each area in turn, eg,

PEOPLE/RELATIONSHIPS 'not enough contact with colleagues' .

Enter NIL in the areas about which you have no complaints.

- In the next column, note a specific example of your complaint. The more specific you can be, the more you will know what needs to be tackled, eg,

PEOPLE/RELATIONSHIPS 'No coffee break – we each take coffee in our own office'.

When you have completed all you wish to in the complaints and examples columns, ask yourself:

> How do I react to seeing what I have written?
>
> How great/small, constant/rare are the causes of my complaints?

> How much are the matters I complain about my responsibility or the responsibility of others?
>
> Are there complaints for which I cannot provide examples? What does this suggest?

COMPLAINTS INTO OBJECTIVES				
Job	Complaints	Examples of complaint	Objectives	Indication of success
People/ Relationships	Not enough contact with colleagues	No coffee break – we each take coffee in our own offices	Organise a social area for coffee breaks	Room 203 set aside with comfortable chairs; coffee urn purchased
Finance				
Prospects				
Activities or tasks	etc.			
Time		etc.		
Surroundings			etc.	
Life-style				etc.
Other				

This exercise was adapted from Loughary and Ripley[13]

The next stage in this exercise is to translate complaints into objectives. Your complaints are comments on 'how things are' at present. Now we would like you to begin to describe 'how I would like things to be'.

Take each complaint in turn and write in the objective column what you would like to do to improve things eg,

PEOPLE/RELATIONSHIPS 'Not enough contact with colleagues'

OBJECTIVE To organise social area for coffee breaks (or to organise, with others, a staff social club).

Try to express each objective in positive terms. Refer to what it is that *you* want to do — setting objectives for somebody else can be very ineffective!

Be specific and include a definite time by which you hope to achieve your objective. Objectives stand more chance of becoming realities if:

- You act positively

- You take responsibility

- You know specifically what you wish to achieve, and by when.

In the last column, try to list an example of what would result if you achieved your objective — ie, what will be a mark of success for you. (Thinking of a specific example can be a check of how realistic are your objectives — if the example looks very remote and unlikely then you may want to review your objectives.)

It is particularly useful to talk through your plans for turning COMPLAINTS into OBJECTIVES with another person. That can be really helpful, since it will:

- encourage you to explore and clarify your dissatisfactions and what you will do about them;

- offer the possibility of a 'contract for change' in which you openly declare your intentions (and are more likely, therefore, to be committed to achieving them);

- invite support for some of the things you wish to do.

Place any objectives you have as a result of this exercise in your 'AHA!' Folder.

It took us so long to discover the black holes in space because we always looked where the light was better — at the stars.

Bob Sample

'No one ever stumbled across anything sitting down.'

Charles Kettering

Keep a record
- Your completed worksheet
- Any objectives you came up with

Rainbow Building Progress Check

WHAT CHANGES DO I WANT?

The last two exercises have provided a way of thinking (in an oblique way) about changes we would like.

> What have I learned from about what I would like to change?

....

....

....

....

....

....

....

....

....

....

....

....

....

....

....

....

We continue with some more exercises designed to open up your thinking about what additional personal changes you might wish to make.

Looking Ahead

Exercise 24: This is your life ... continued*

Data needed

• Your lifeline from Exercise 1

• Return to the 'Drawing my lifeline' exercise you completed on page 24. That exercise stopped at the point you have reached now. We want you to continue your lifeline

   – AS YOU WOULD WISH IT TO CONTINUE ...

Add as many details as you can of your life ahead as you would want it to be. Then reflect on these questions.

> Is this in any way different from how I think it *will* continue? In what ways?
>
> What might prevent me from getting the lifeline that I want?

> Which constraints can I do something about and which do I think I could do little or nothing about?

> How many of the impediments stem from factors outside my control, and how many might emanate from within myself?
>
> What can I do to get more of what matters to me?

Keep a record

• Your new life line
• Notes

Exercise 25: Let me introduce myself

This is a verbal alternative to the last exercise, which in its own way can be equally challenging because we have to verbalise our thinking to another person.

• Find a colleague with whom you can do this exercise.

• First, take 10 minutes to introduce yourself to your friend as you are now. Having completed the section on WHO AM I? you should have plenty to talk about!

• Next, spend 5-10 minutes introducing yourself as the person you were exactly 10 years ago. This is more powerful if you speak in the first person – as if it really was you but ten years younger.

• Finally, spend 5-10 minutes introducing yourself as the person living the life you think is most likely ten years from now. Again, try to keep it in the first person.

> Which of these introductions did I find most difficult?
> Why?

> Is there a difference between what I hope my life will be like ten years from now and what I realistically think it will be ten years from now?

> What are the implications of this for my future decision-making?

Keep a record

• Notes about the way you described yourself in the future

Exercise 26: My life roles in my future

On page 26, you completed an analysis of what proportion of time you are spending on your range of life roles.

- Imagine yourself as you think you are most likely to be in ten years from now. Write down what you would see yourself being and doing for each life role.

Data needed

- Your analysis of life roles from Exercise 2

Keep a record

- Notes about the way you described yourself in the future

Exercise 27: My obituary*

RAINBOW BUILDING SKILL: *Knowing yourself*
Learning from experience

Newspapers publish obituaries which give a description of a person's life-history, achievements, key relationships, etc., plus an evaluation of the person's life.

• Write your obituary† as an objective journalist might do it, including the time and manner of your death. It should not be more than 500-600 words.

After you have completed your obituary, ask yourself these questions:

> How would I summarise that person's life? Can I think of a suitable epitaph?
>
> Write it here.

> How might I have liked that obituary to read differently?
> What can I now do to ensure that my obituary will read like I would want it to read?

MY OBITUARY

....
....
....
....
....
....
....
....
....
....
....
....
....
....
....
....
....
....
....

---

†Some people experienced difficulty and distress in completing this exercise, but eventually they have found it of great value. As with all other exercises, do not do it if it does not feel right for you!

Rainbow Building Progress Check

WHAT CHANGES DO I WANT?

What have I learned about the sort of future I would like for myself?

....

....

....

....

....

....

....

....

....

....

....

....

....

....

....

....

....

What Stops You From Getting What You Want?

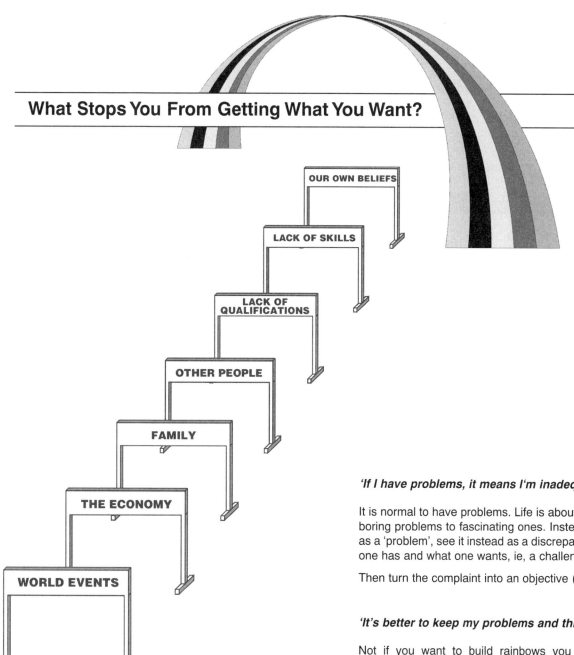

OUR OWN BELIEFS

LACK OF SKILLS

LACK OF QUALIFICATIONS

OTHER PEOPLE

FAMILY

THE ECONOMY

WORLD EVENTS

'If I have problems, it means I'm inadequate'

It is normal to have problems. Life is about progressing from boring problems to fascinating ones. Instead of thinking of it as a 'problem', see it instead as a discrepancy between what one has and what one wants, ie, a challenge!

Then turn the complaint into an objective (Page 102).

'It's better to keep my problems and thinking to myself'

Not if you want to build rainbows you don't! There are genuine personality differences to consider here. Some people like to talk just about everything through with others, while others prefer to work through an issue by themselves. The research findings on problem-solving, however, are very clear. The quality of problem-solving is almost always improved by involving other people's contributions.

There may be times when we need to be alone to sort things out, but any conclusion or decision will undoubtedly benefit from discussing it at some point with people who you know are useful resources and providers of feedback.

'I cannot live on less than I earn now'

In our experience, this is hardly ever the case. What is required is a careful identification of present income and expenditure matched alongside priorities. Test this out for yourself with Exercise 28.

The hurdles designed to prevent us from getting what we want

Some of these hurdles are outside our control, for example, world events and the economy; some are partially under cur control, for example, the influence that we allow our family and other people to have over us, and lacking qualifications and skills; some are totally under our own control, namely, the beliefs that we have about ourselves and the attitudes we have developed.

Let us examine some of the beliefs that we have found can be blocks to RAINBOW BUILDING.

- Prepare a budget sheet for you or your family.

  We reproduce below an example of a typical budget sheet†, but don' think that you must use this one as it stands. It may not fit for you. Feel free to design your own.

BUDGET SHEET					
INCOME	AMOUNT		OUTGOINGS		AMOUNT
Wages/salary			Money	Savings	
Building society interest				Interest charges	
Child allowance			Property	Rent/mortgage	
Any perks, e.g. company car,				Rates	
cheap house loan, etc.				Insurance	
Other			Car and other travel	(Re)payments	
				Tax	
				Insurance	
				Fares: work	
				other	
				AA/RAC	
				Petrol, oil	
				Servicing, repairs	
			Food	All food	
				Meals out (inc. school)	
				Alcohol	
			Appliances	(Re)payments	
				TV licence & rental	
				Servicing, repairs	
			Holidays	Travel	
				Accommodation	
				Other	
			Household expenses	Gas	
				Electricity	
				Phone	
				Cleaning materials	
				Cleaning, repairs	
				Other	
			Entertainment and leisure	Newspapers	
				Meals/shows	
				Sports	
				DIY materials	
				Garden	
				Subscriptions	
				Children's lessons	
				Other	
			Furnishing	Furniture	
				Soft furnishings	
			Clothing	Clothes, shoes	
			Miscellaneous	Birthdays. Xmas	
				Tobacco	
				Life insurance	
				Hairdresser	
				Other	
TOTAL			TOTAL		

†Adapted from *Consumer Decisions,* with permission from the Open University

For this kind of analysis, you can begin to determine what you absolutely must have to live, as opposed to what you would choose to have.

For example:

- you could sell your car and travel by public transport.

- you may need a house but could you sell your existing one for a profit and buy a cheaper one?

- you may need a holiday but how about a home-exchange plan, or self-catering instead of a hotel?

Before you say 'Well, that takes all the fun out of life!', remember that we are looking here at what is absolutely necessary.

> What have I eliminated?
>
> Can I gain satisfactions provided by those items elsewhere or in a cheaper way?

For example, stop eating out so much and experiment with a new cooking cuisine at home.

Buy fewer books and make more use of the public library.

> If I were starting up again, just what would I need? (You can strip away the present accoutrements and expectations you have developed over the years.)
>
> Do I really still need all the income that I have? What are the implications of this?

One conclusion from this could also be that this confirms for you that you have insufficient income. Your issue would then be to generate some alternatives to acquire extra income. (See Resources Section on page 147.)

> **Keep a record**
>
> - Your budget sheet and analysis

'I can't live without...

money
status
a particular person
my work
etc?'

Many of us trap ourselves into a lifestyle because of assumptions we make of what we must have before life is worthwhile. Our hunger can sometimes be so consuming that we pursue goals which clearly are not in our own best interests. In some parts of the world where people enjoy monkey meat, they have developed a novel way of trapping monkeys. A coconut is hollowed out through a small hole in the shell. Boiled rice, which monkeys apparently adore, is placed inside the hole which is just big enough for an average sized monkeyfist to squeeze through. The shell is tied to a tree. Now, when the greedy monkey discovers the shell and the rice, he also discovers that he can just get his hand inside the shell, but as soon as he takes a handful of rice, he cannot get his hand out again! The monkey, you might predict would drop the rice to escape. But instead, he cannot bring himself to let go and sits watching the hunters come closer and closer until they club him to death. Most of us have our own monkey traps: things, ideas, people that we cannot let go of even if it means our stultifying and perhaps dying, psychologically and even physically (eg, with stress-related diseases). We must have material possessions, or security of job, or the permanence of a relationship at all costs, or a belief of how the world should be as opposed to how it is. Looked at this way, perhaps it is easier to understand just how a monkey can be so stupid!

Exercise 28: My monkey trap

RAINBOW BUILDING SKILL: Knowing yourself

- Thinking through the story of the monkey trap, write down an equivalent trap in your life.

> What is my rice?
> What could I gain if I let go of my rice?
> Are there different kinds of rice?

> Is the trap the only place I can find rice?
> Is there more than one kind of rice?
> Is the rice actually worth risking my life?
> What is holding on to the rice costing me?

> **Keep a record**
>
> - Your description
> - Your thoughts on how to avoid The trap

'It is undignified to have to promote or sell oneself'

This relates to a huge myth, namely, that talents will always be spotted. Our experiences suggest that talents first have to be put on show.

Why should anyone have confidence in you unless you give them some evidence for it? Exercise 30 will invite you to do this.

Of course, you cannot provide that evidence unless you have it. That is why your answers to Question 1: WHO AM I? are so crucial.

'Somewhere in the world there is THE JOB waiting for me'

From Section 1, you should have discovered that for your interests, skills and values, there will be many jobs that you could do and would probably be very happy doing.

In the UK alone there are some 23 million jobs and 3,000 occupational titles.

To a large extent, too, a job is what you can make of it. Jobs are not like ready-to-wear clothes that you have to fit yourself into. While there will always be limits to the pattern, to a certain extent you can always cut some of your own cloth.

'The job I have now is ideal and therefore it always will be'

We have already discussed the rapid rate of technological change which means that in the unlikely event of your staying exactly the same, the chances of your job staying the same (or even just staying) are minimal.

Just as new needs develop as old needs are satisfied (see page 48) for our lives in general, so is the case with jobs.

An American research study[6] has shown that a person's needs from a job change over time. To begin with, job security and safety are vital – just making sure that you are seen to be competent enough to hold the job down. Next comes the need to be accepted and to have one's work recognised. During these stages, too much autonomy and challenge may actually prevent you from performing at your best. These factors assume greater importance only after your more basic needs are met.

The same research showed clearly that after 15 years or so, even the most enriching job tends to becoming boring.

The message for us here is that we must periodically review what we are getting out of our jobs, and that we should not get angry with ourselves or worry if we become dissatisfied with what we nave previously found satisfying. That is what life is about. It is called DEVELOPMENT.

'Whatever I do or plan is useless. It will all eventually be determined by my firm/my family/the Government...'

There will always be factors out of our control, but many things are open to our influence. In the final analysis, we always have control over our own reactions to any event or decision. We can create unnecessary frustration by assuming that we can or should be able to influence everything.

You cannot change the world but you might be able to change your bit of it.

'Somewhere in the world, there is the PERSONNEL MANAGER, FIRM or BOSS who will discover me and my potential'

How? Not unless we make ourselves known, communicate our skills and qualities and market ourselves as a desirable product. If we can't be bothered to advertise ourselves, why should anyone else be interested enough to do it for us?

Exercise 30: Buy me today

- Imagine yourself to be a product. Your task is to launch this new product successfully.

  To sell any product successfully, you need to believe in it. To believe in it, you need to know just what it is capable of, but also any deficiencies or problems there might be with it, because you, as the sales person, will be held accountable.

  We would like you to produce:

  –   a 'product analysis' on yourself,

  –   an assessment of your development needs,

  –   an appropriate sales slogan, if you were to promote yourself as a 'product',

  –   a rationale explaining why somebody should buy a 'product' like you.

  Enter these items on the Table opposite. The Table includes sample responses from some of our participants to show how the exercise might be completed.

> **Keep a record**
> - Your product specifications
> - An advert for yourself

'It's unethical to think of people in terms of how helpful they might be to my career'

Using people as resources is not the same as 'using' people in some manipulative way especially if we are also open to be used as resources by others.

People are invaluable for information, for support and sometimes for advice. Armed with specific questions, you can learn more about a job or a leisure pursuit in 30-60 minutes from a well-informed person than from spending 6 hours in a library.

One of the most valuable things you can do in searching out job opportunities and leisure options is to 'plug' yourself in to networks of people.

We so often fail to ask for help from the human resources that are all around us and at our disposal.

Exercise 31: Who do I know?

RAINBOW BUILDING SKILL: Research skills.

- List the names of relatives, your friends, your colleagues (check your address book). These need not be people who are immediately obvious as useful contacts. List the names for their purpose may only become apparent later.

  You will probably have at least 100 names by now. This is your PERSONAL CONTACT NETWORK.

  Yet each of these people has a PERSONAL CONTACT NETWORK of their own, which gives you access to 5-10,000 people even allowing for overlap between networks.

- Begin to analyse your own network.

  - What jobs are represented?

  - What interests?

  - What skills?

  - What special knowledge?

- What are the strengths/opportunities provided by my network to help me in my career and life planning?

- How could I make more use of my network?

Note: One theory about the value of networks in job seeking says, 'Never ask people directly to help you (they may feel put on the spot), but make them aware of your interests and talents and ask them to bear you in mind please!'

Keep a record

- Your network

Narrowing down your objectives

Exercise 32: More of...., less of.... matrix*

RAINBOW BUILDING SKILL: Objective setting

This matrix is one that many participants on our workshops have found to be useful for collecting together all the possible areas for personal change that the rainbow building process has identified thus far. If you find that it inhibits you rather than facilitates you, don't use it. You will need to find an alternative way of collecting up your personal data to enable you to decide which areas of your life require some action.

- Using the Matrix set out on page 114, identify in each category what you would like more of, or less of, in terms of contact with particular PEOPLE or in terms of the things you spend time on, ACTIVITIES. (The central column, 'Keep the Same', can be used to register what is satisfactory at present and you may find it useful to enter details in that section also.) The more specific you can be in your entries, the more useful they are likely to be at the next stage. Produce your own matrix on a large sheet of paper if this one is not large enough.

  An sample set of entries for the heading 'Your Present Job' is provided at the top of the page, to show how to go about filling in the form.

- When you have filled in the form, circle the three things that you would most like to do something about.

MORE OF...., LESS OF.... MATRIX				
		MORE OF	KEEP THE SAME	LESS OF
Your Present Job	People			
	Activities			
Your Career	People			
	Activities			
Your Life in General	People			
	Activities			

EXAMPLE				
		MORE OF	KEEP THE SAME	LESS OF
Your Present Job	People	*Contact with colleagues doing similar work*	*The amount of contact time with clients (as distinct from staff)*	*Staff bringing issues for me to confirm decisions they have already taken*
	Activities	*Creative forward planning new ideas sessions*	*Amount of responsibility and supervision of others' work*	*Routine paperwork*

Rainbow Building Summary Sheet

WHAT CHANGES DO I WANT?

What have I learned from my FANTASIES about what changes I want in my life?

From my LIFE REVIEW and MY LIFE CHOICES exercises I know that I want to change...

What OBJECTIVES do I have arising from my COMPLAINTS?

What stops me getting what I want?

Do I want to do anything about it, and if so, what?

What is my own ADVERTISING SLOGAN?

What 3 things do I want MORE OF or LESS OF?

Question 5
HOW DO I MAKE THEM HAPPEN?

The key to getting more of what you want, to making things more like you want them to be, is likely to be the precision with which you can SET OBJECTIVES and MAKE ACTION PLANS. Failure to achieve much of what we would like in life can be traced to one or all of the following:

- low motivation,
- unclear objectives,
- ill-formed action plans.

We are assuming that, like all RAINBOW BUILDERS, you will be motivated to work for what you want, so we would now like you to give attention to clarifying your objectives and identifying the steps you will take to achieve them.

ROUTE MAP
for "How do I make them happen?"

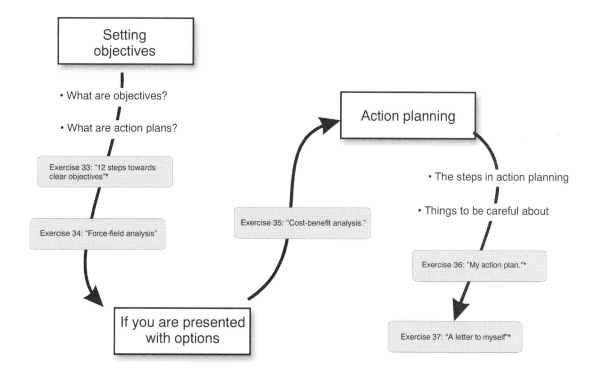

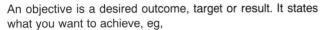

Setting Objectives

An objective is a desired outcome, target or result. It states what you want to achieve, eg,

'I want to get a job which involves less stress and gives me more free time.'

Objectives are important in defining what we want, in giving us a sense of direction, in offering us a chance to shape our own development.

IF YOU DON'T KNOW WHERE YOU ARE GOING,
YOU WILL PROBABLY END UP
SOMEWHERE ELSE!

An objective states simply what we want to achieve, it does not describe tasks or activities which we will undertake to achieve it – those will be part of your ACTION PLAN to achieve your objectives. For example, 'I will buy a selection of newspapers to look for job vacancies', is part of an action plan.

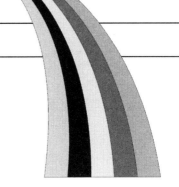

Many men go fishing all of their lives without knowing that it is not the fish they are after.

Paul Thoreau

Exercise 33: 12 steps towards clear objectives*

RAINBOW BUILDING SKILL: ***Objective setting***
Action planning
Making decisions

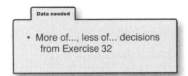

Data needed

• More of..., less of... decisions from Exercise 32

• Refer back to your MORE OF ... LESS OF ... MATRIX, or whatever summary sheet you have used.

• Write down on separate pieces of paper each of the 3 objectives you wish to do something about.

• For each objective, take the following steps. Write down your answers. At the end of this process you should have defined at least 3 clear objectives.

1. State your objective clearly – start with the word 'To ...' followed by an action word. For example: 'To work for promotion to Head of Department in my present job.'

2. Ask yourself whether there is an objective behind your objective. Ask why you want what you want – there may be other ways of getting it, for example, if you are pursuing responsibility, status or extra money, there may be other ways of achieving it without actually being promoted.

3. State clearly how you will know when your objective has been reached – this will ensure that your objective is clear.

4. Make your objective as specific as possible, for example, not 'I want my life to be more rewarding' ... but, 'I want to get more satisfaction from my job by replacing some of the paperwork with time to do creative forward planning.'

5. State when you want to achieve this by, and why you choose that date. For example; 'I want to achieve promotion by this time next year, because to wait longer would be frustrating.'

6. Be clear for whom you want this. If it is not for yourself, will the other person find the objective acceptable? Is this relevant?

7. Check whether any of your objectives conflict. For example, if you have said that you want to work for promotion to Head of Department but also that you want to spend more time with your family, then you have to decide whether these two objectives are compatible. If any of your objectives conflict, then you will obviously have to identify which ones have priority and work on those.

8. Identify any constraints (external or internal) which will make your objective more difficult to achieve.

9. Identify any resources (external or internal) which will assist the achievement of your objective.

10. Check that your objective is realistic – as before, talking it through with someone else (or with several other people) can provide useful alternative perspectives on how to tackle it.

11. Ask whether there is anything to stop you achieving your objective now. If not, you are ready to start. But if there are obstacles, then obviously you have as an initial objective to work to overcome those particular constraints.

12. How do you feel about what you have just decided to do? You may need someone who will give you real support while you work on achieving your objective.

This process can be repeated for any number of objectives.

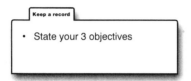

Keep a record

• State your 3 objectives

Exercise 34: Force-field analysis

RAINBOW BUILDING SKILL: *Making decisions*
                                      Objective setting and
                                      Action planning

Force-field analysis is a way of improving your chances of achieving an objective or an action plan. It can be a method for examining what is involved in changes we may be thinking of making, and of identifying which forces may be helpful in making the changes, or which may work against the changes.

The method was developed by Kurt Lewin to demonstrate efficient and inefficient ways of achieving personal change.

In any situation where we wish to make a change, there will always be some forces at work assisting us and some forces at work resisting us.

For example:

Emma and Bill live in London. They both have good, well paid jobs. They have always talked of moving to the country, away from the city and nearer to Emma's parents who are getting older. Bill is not happy in his present job and had found a business close to where her parents live which he wants them to take on together. Emma, however, has excellent career prospects and does not want to give up now. How then does Bill attempt to create conditions which will render Emma more open to change? A typical approach is to extol the virtues of the new scheme, the chance of living in the country, of getting away from the rat-race of the city and be near enough to her parents to visit more often. However, using this approach is more likely to increase resistance to any move than to inspire Emma to join him.

The following diagram represents the forces working for and against Emma's acceptance of this move.

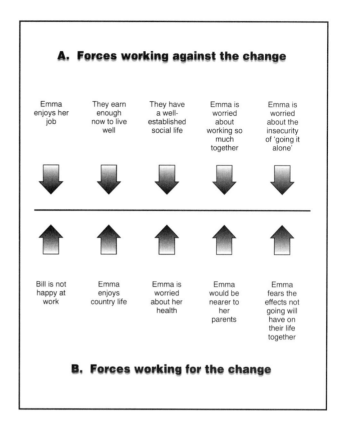

The approaches that Bill has tried have all been concerned with reinforcing the upward pressures, namely emphasising the beneficial effects a move could have for him, their lifestyle and her parents.

However, our model is something of a physical one, and every physicist knows that if the forces operating on an object in a state of equilibrium are increased in one direction, then the forces in the opposite direction must increase equally if the equilibrium is to be maintained. This means that our arrows now look like this:

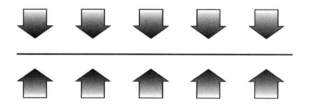

What has happened is that forces operating on each side are now significantly stronger, and tension is at a higher level,

Emma's frustration will increase, and her resistance is likely to harden.

What happens if Bill uses the other alternative open to him and concentrates on the downward forces (A) that make Emma resistant to change? This approach is called reducing resistance. If Bill tackles her concerns about the scheme and succeeds in reducing her resistance, then a new equilibrium is reached, but at a lower level of tension.

This is like stopping a car by taking one's foot off the accelerator, without using the brake.

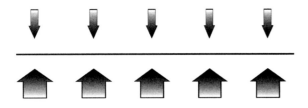

The following exercise invites you to use this approach, alongside the more traditional one of building on the forces working for change.

The technique is to:

1. Identify your objective.

   • State what you want to achieve, very specifically using the word 'To ...', and include when you hope to achieve it (ie, 'by ...')

   • Make sure you have stated only one objective. Deal with them one at a time!

2. List the forces working IN FAVOUR of what you want to achieve.

   • A positive force is anything which will contribute to your achieving your objective.

   • When listing forces, be very specific (i.e. what, who, where, when, how much, how many, etc) Remember these forces may be inside or outside you.

   • Indicate how the force will contribute to your achieving what you want.

3. List all the forces working AGAINST what you want to achieve.

   • Again, be specific.

   • List all factors, inside or outside yourself which will work against you.

   • Indicate what effect each force is likely to have on your achieving your objective.

4. Analyse the forces.

   • Identify which forces are most important, (these will be real, not assumed, and will have a significant effect on whether or not you can achieve your objective).

   • Circle all the important forces on your list.

   • Obtain any additional information you feel you may lack about any important force.

5. Weaken the negative – strengthen the positive.

   • Work on each important force in turn.

   • Identify ways in which you can reduce, minimise or eliminate (not exterminate!) each force working against you. Indicate any that you really cannot find a way of reducing by writing 'no action possible' against it.

   • Identify ways in which you can increase, strengthen, or maximise each positive force. Work on one at a time.

6. Assess how feasible your objective or action plan seems to be.

   Ask yourself: Do the positives clearly outweigh the negatives or will they when I have maximised and minimised them?

   • If the answer is 'yes', ask yourself again 'Do I really want to achieve this?'

   • If the answer again is 'yes', adopt your objective and begin to work on these forces.

   • If the answer is 'no', then your choice is to abandon it or change it. For example, it may be possible to modify the original by reducing your sights or revising the target time.

If You Are Presented With Options

Exercise 35: Cost-benefit analysis

It can be useful in helping us to choose between different options to see represented the COSTS and the BENEFITS of each option.

- Write down the options you wish to consider, for example:

  - to wait for promotion in my present job.

  - to seek a more senior job in a similar department in another company.

  - to seek to transfer to another department in my present company and change my direction.

- Write the first option at the top of a sheet of paper. Divide the page down the middle and head the column on the left COSTS and the one on the right BENEFITS. (see diagram below). Enter in the COSTS column any disadvantages you (or you and others) can think of if you were to pursue that option. When you have finished listing all the COSTS you can think of, read back through the list. Attempt to grade each cost on a 1 to 10 scale as an indication of how you feel about the prospect eg, 1 if you think it is a very slight disadvantage, 10 if it feels to be a major disadvantage to you. Score the rest in between.

- Finally, put a circle round the two biggest disadvantages.

- Place your cost/benefit balance sheets alongside each other.

- Examine, think about or talk through your reactions to looking at each sheet again.

- Ask yourself, or identify, whether any option seems on balance to give you most of what you want.

- If it does, decide whether the costs of it are acceptable to you. If so, begin to make it happen!

- If there is no option which is clearly better for you than another, then you have to choose either (a) to postpone the decision or (b) risk choosing one option when there is no convincing indicator.

- Write down, or declare what you have decided.

N.B. It can be useful sometimes to think through 'What happens if I do nothing, or fail to make a decision?' — sometimes the consequences of inertia are not considered!

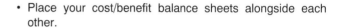

Keep a record

- The results of your cost-benefit Analysis

COST-BENEFIT ANALYSIS (EXAMPLE)

OPTION: Waiting for promotion

COSTS	RATING	BENEFITS	RATING
No change of scene	2	I know the job and can do it well	(7)
No change of people	5	Little stress	3
Lack of challenge	8	The company knows my strengths	3
May wait in vain	8	I need not move house	(8)
Feeling helpless	(9)		
Someone else might beat me to it	(9)		

- Move now to the BENEFITS column under your first option and list any gains you might make from choosing that option. Grade the benefits on a 1 to 10 scale as an indication of how much a gain you feel it would be eg, 1 if it feels only slightly advantageous, 10 if it feels to be highly advantageous to you. Score the rest in between. Finally put a circle round the two most attractive advantages from your point of view.

Repeat this process for each option!

Rainbow Building Progress Check

HOW DO I MAKE THEM HAPPEN?

Using the techniques outlined, collect together all your objectives and make them as clear as possible. Look back through your AHA! Folder.

....
....
....
....
....
....
....
....
....
....
....
....
....
....
....
....
....

Action Planning

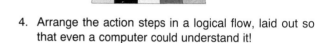

When you have a clearly defined OBJECTIVE, the next step is to develop an ACTION PLAN.

An ACTION PLAN provides you with the answer to the question:

'What do I do to achieve my objective?'

The steps in ACTION PLANNING are as follows:

1. Have a clearly defined objective.

   Too many action plans fail because the objective is not clear enough in the first place.

2. Start with what YOU are going to do NOW.

   The diagram below graphically portrays how action plans can get lost in the swamp, if you try to change too much or plan too far ahead.

3. Be very specific about the steps you will take to achieve your objective.

   For example, not, 'I'll have a chat with my boss' .. but, 'I will try to see my boss on Thursday to discuss my current job performance and ask about ways in which I might get promotion.'

4. Arrange the action steps in a logical flow, laid out so that even a computer could understand it!

5. Be aware that one action step will often involve you in planning a prior one. For example: 'I will telephone the boss's secretary this afternoon to arrange an appointment for Thursday morning.'

6. Decide when you will review your progress and write this into your action plan.

7. Transfer your plan to a diary to remind you of the particular dates by which the steps need to have been completed.

   Contracting with others is particularly useful to ensure that you are sticking to an action plan.

8. Always be prepared to change the plan as circumstances change or if some of your steps do not turn out as you have wished.

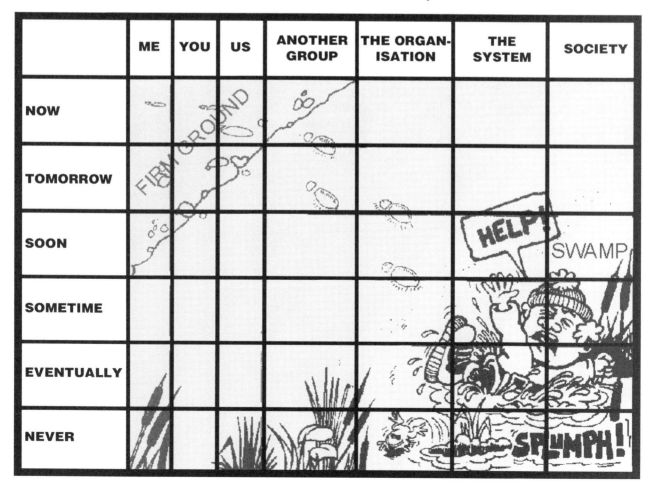

	ME	YOU	US	ANOTHER GROUP	THE ORGAN-ISATION	THE SYSTEM	SOCIETY
NOW							
TOMORROW							
SOON							
SOMETIME							
EVENTUALLY							
NEVER							

Exercise 36: My action plan*

RAINBOW BUILDING SKILL: ***Objective setting and Action planning.***

Take one of your objectives and develop an ACTION PLAN for it.

- My objective is:

  ....
  ....
  ....
  ....
  ....
  ....
  ....

- List the most useful action steps, without worrying about their sequence.

  What I need to do is:

  ....
  ....
  ....
  ....
  ....
  ....

- Number them according to which comes first. Then complete the following timetable:

  I am going to start with Step 1 on .... *(give date)*

  I am going to start with Step 2 on .... *(give date)*

  I will review my progress on .... *(give date)*

  I should know whether my objective has been reached or not by .... *(give date)*

GOOD LUCK! AND DON'T GET LOST IN THE SWAMP

You can now return to your other objectives and produce action plans for them.

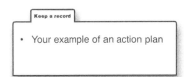

Keep a record

- Your example of an action plan

Exercise 37: A letter to myself*

To:
The Rainbow Builder

Not to be opened until .... (a date six months ahead)

- A particularly effective method of reviewing progress is, at this stage, to write a letter to yourself.

- Spell out clearly what you hope to have achieved for each of your priority objectives in the six months after writing the letter.

  To save time you may wish to send yourself a photocopy of the summary sheet on the next page. We, personally, prefer the flexibility (and informality) of a separately drafted letter.

- Give the letter to someone who could be relied upon to post it to you exactly six months to the day after you have written it. By then you will, most likely, have forgotten all about it. Its appearance on your doormat can generate feelings ranging from delight to despair as you see just how far you have achieved, or moved towards achieving, your objectives.

Rainbow Building Summary Sheet

HOW DO I MAKE THEM HAPPEN?

My major OBJECTIVES are: *(in order of priority)*	To be achieved by:	ACTION PLAN? *(tick if you have one)*

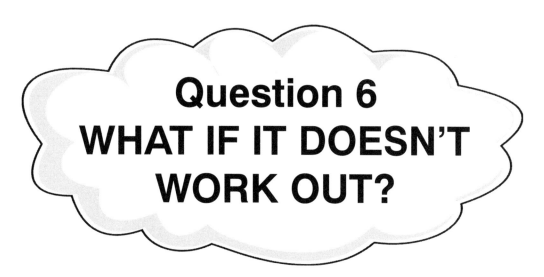

Question 6
WHAT IF IT DOESN'T WORK OUT?

We suggested earlier that, as you worked through the first five questions, there might be times when it would be appropriate to turn to Question 6. As you worked through the exercises you may have felt frustration over the constraints in your life which restrict your options or make the changes you want to bring about more difficult. Perhaps you felt disappointment over past opportunities missed. Even if you did find the exercises stimulating and constructive, you will still need the lifeskills of coping when things don't work out for use in the rest of your life.

ROUTE MAP

for "What If It Doesn't Work Out?"

Coping With Disappointment

'When I finally got the means to an end, they moved the ends further apart.'

Sam Levinson

However clear our objectives and specific our action plans, however much time and energy we invest, there are always some factors outside our control which could result in our not getting what we want.

In addition, we do make mistakes! Our aims might not be realistic, our skills insufficiently developed, or we may even change our minds!

Taking the risk of succeeding requires us also to take the risk of failing. The alternative would seem to be to sit tight and let life happen to us. That way we can stay out of the rain-storm but we won't have a chance to build a rainbow.

Although we can, through successful career and life management, keep our disappointments to a minimum, we cannot expect all of our plans and projects to succeed. And when a disappointment does occur, it can be inappropriate to tell someone, 'We can learn more from our mistakes than from our successes'. When our plans do not work out, we need to sound off about our feelings of disappointment, frustration and anger. Yet, most people do discover in the long run that they can learn a great deal by looking back and analysing what went wrong and considering alternative steps they could have taken or recognising the skills they lacked at the time.

It is helpful to acknowledge that not all of our plans will work out and to have suitable strategies ready for coping at these times.

We avoid using the word failure because too many people apply the word to themselves rather than to their plans. It can be helpful to recognise 'Yes, this particular plan of mine failed', but it's extremely self destructive to think, 'I am a failure because my plan didn't work out'!

When you reach a point at which you realise things are not working out you need to consider two questions:

• How can I cope with the disappointment?

• What else can I try?

When a plan doesn't work out there are two areas a RAINBOW BUILDER has to manage:

EMOTIONAL

and

RATIONAL

The alternative strategies we suggest later are all very well if you are feeling strong and rational but that is often the last thing you feel when you have to face a major disappointment.

The emotional reactions, for most people, will have to be dealt with first.

> How do you feel when faced with great disappointment?

• Think back to a particular disappointment in your life. It may help to write down the details.

• Recall your first reactions – how did you feel? – what did you feel like doing?

• To what extent were these the typical feelings you have in response to disappointments?

• Now think about what you actually do at these times. List the typical things that you do when you face disappointment.

Coping with disappointment will usually involve one or a combination of:

– Getting rid of bad feelings.

– Having someone to talk to.

– Talking constructively to yourself.

– Looking after yourself under stress.

Look back at your responses above. Which of these four did you use?

1. Getting rid of bad feelings.

Crying, shouting, beating a cushion, digging the garden, going for a run or a swim, playing squash are all common ways in which people do this. Keeping these feelings inside you or worse still not being able to admit to yourself that disappointment generates bad feelings all add to the building up of stress and make the disappointment more difficult to cope with. Now that you've thought about it a bit more, do the ways you typically cope with disappointment allow you to get rid of the bad feelings? Which of these suggestions might you try another time? Can you think of others that might particularly suit you?

2. Having someone to talk to.

A problem for many of us is that we often expect most of our support and emotional sustenance from one or two people. We sometimes act as if it is wholly reasonable to expect to get all of our needs satisfied by a single person – usually a spouse or partner, or one's immediate family, or by one or two close friends. The following exercise will help you to identify just who is in your support network whilst making the point that support is a many-faceted thing. You do have a choice to extend it, plug gaps, make changes.

RAINBOW BUILDING SKILL: Looking After Yourself

Write in the names of people you know who provide you with these different kinds of support in your job and away from your job.

MY SUPPORT NETWORK		
TYPES OF SUPPORT	AT MY JOB	AWAY FROM MY JOB
Someone I can always rely on		
Someone I just enjoy chatting to		
Someone with whom I can discuss the exercises in this book		
Someone who makes me feel competent and valued		
Someone who gives me constructive feedback		
Someone who is always a valuable source of information		
Someone who will challenge me to sit up and take a good look at myself		
Someone I can depend upon in a crisis		
Someone I can feel close to – a friend or intimate		
Someone I can share bad news with		
Someone I can share good news and good feelings with		
Someone who introduces me to new ideas, new interests, new people		

> Does anything surprise me when I look at the extent of my support network?

> Are there any gaps?

> Do I rely on only one or two people for my support?
>
> Does this matter? What are the consequences of this for me and for them?

> Do I wish to change my support network in any way?

Your answers to the last question should be kept with your previous work on Question 3: 'What changes do I want?' in your AHA! FOLDER.

It is sometimes difficult to feel that you can ask for support.

However, most people are happy to offer this kind of support. It helps, too, if you make a practice of seeking support rather than bottling things up. Then you will not find it so difficult to approach people when you do have to cope with major disappointments. For most people, offering support is a two-way process: they willingly give support and hope to receive it when they need it.

Some people feel it's important to keep their problems to themselves and manage on their own so as not to bother other people. But since most people like to be asked for help when it's really needed, such an attitude could be seen as either misplaced pride or as a signal that the person, underneath his pride, feels he is not worth bothering about or doesn't deserve help.

If you find it difficult to identify people to whom you could turn, go back to the 'Personal Contact Network' you drew up in Exercise 31 and check through to find those, not in your immediate close circle of friends, who could offer appropriate support if you asked them.

> **Keep a record**
> - Your support network
> - Observations and action plans

It's always possible that, because of the nature of the problem, or because you are away from home or have moved, that you may not be able to think of anyone who could help. In this case, a local Citizens Advice Bureau can suggest sources of voluntary or professional help.

Remember too that the Samaritans (any telephone operator will give you the local number) advertise that they offer a 'Listening ear' service around the clock. They also know where else you might seek help. You may be most unlikely ever to need this type of help but knowing that it exists and how to make use of it is a valuable lifeskill and would ensure that you would know how to cope if the occasion did arise.

3. Talking constructively to yourself

We will spend some time examining this skill because it is so crucial to us when things do not turn out well for us. The way we think is likely to have a highly significant influence on the way we feel and what we do. The way in which we perceive a given situation, what we 'tell ourselves' as we think about it, will have a decisive effect on what feelings we experience and on our actions which follow as a consequence.

Typically, when some unfortunate event or experience happens to us, we feel bad. We assume that our bad feelings are created by that event, ie,

EVENT ⇨ BAD FEELINGS

What actually happens, however, is that something comes between the EVENT and the FEELINGS which will determine just what kind of feelings we experience. That 'something' we call SELF-TALK. This determines how we experience any EVENT, which in turn will determine what we FEEL and ultimately our ACTIONS.

The real sequence, therefore, is:

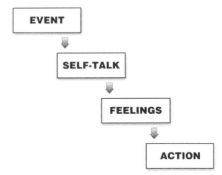

For example: This was one person's reaction to having failed a driving test:

EVENT:	This person's objective was to pass his driving test and he failed.
SELF-TALK:	'I'm pathetic. Anyone can pass a driving test. I'm a failure. I'm not risking being made to look stupid again."
FEELINGS:	He felt ashamed, frustrated, pathetic.

This is how it can affect, in turn, the fourth factor in our equation:

ACTIONS:	He felt so anxious not to experience those feelings again, he was determined not to put himself at risk. He was not going to try again.

All of this stems from assuming that your FEELINGS are caused directly by the EVENT, whereas they are determined almost totally by how you talk to yourself and interpret the event.

Before the FEELINGS stage, the person above could substitute the following SELF-TALK:

'I am disappointed. It would have been good to have passed, especially as I practised so hard. However, things don't always turn out as we wish. I have failed but that doesn't make me a failure. I have to see what I can learn from my mistakes so that next time I won't make them again.'

Look back to what you said you did when facing disappointment (page 128). Did you use negative self-talk then? If so, what might you have said that would be more positive?

It is important, therefore, in terms of looking after ourselves to realise that:

• What we think will decide what we feel and what we do

• If we can exercise more control over what we think we can manage our feelings and our behaviour more effectively.

• If we do this we can take greater charge of ourselves and the situations we meet.

Realising this is the first step to beginning to learn the kind of 'Self-talk' which will promote looking after ourselves and will reduce the likelihood of our being 'victims' of bad feelings or of situations we cannot control.

Exercise 39: Avoiding self-defeating beliefs

RAINBOW BUILDING SKILL: Communicating

Contrary to what we often believe, other people or things do not make us unhappy. We make ourselves unhappy by what we tell ourselves. We need to train ourselves to avoid negative or destructive self-talk and particularly to avoid thoughts which are based on self-defeating beliefs. These beliefs set up expectations in us of ourselves, of other people, or of the world, which are unrealistic and invite disappointment.

These beliefs lead to most of the feelings of worry, anger, fear, jealousy, depression and guilt that people experience. If we believe them, we will think in terms of 'Things should be ....'. or, 'People ought to be ....' and we will get angry or disappointed a great deal of the time when events or people do not live up to our expectations. If we can begin to accept that there are no 'Shoulds' and 'Oughts' and begin to think in terms of 'It would be preferable if ......', or 'I may need to work to bring that about', then we will be more likely to act to make things more like we want them to be.

Set out opposite is a list of some of the beliefs which are likely to produce problems, if our thinking is based on them. As you read the list, circle the number in front of any to which you always or sometimes subscribe.

PROBLEM-CAUSING BELIEFS

1 I must be loved or liked by everyone, people should love me.

2 I must be perfect in all I do.

3 All the people with whom I work or live must be perfect.

4 I can have little control over what happens to me.

5 It is easier to avoid facing difficulties than to deal with them.

6 Disagreement and conflict are a disaster and must be avoided at all costs.

7 People, including me, do not change.

8 Some people are always good, others are always bad.

9 The world should be perfect and it is terrible and unbearable that it is not.

10 People are fragile and need to be protected from 'the truth'.

11 Other people exist to make us happy and we cannot be happy unless they do so.

12 Crises are invariably and entirely destructive and no good can come of them.

13 Somewhere there is the 'perfect job', the perfect 'solution', the 'perfect partner', etc. and all we need do is search for them.

14 We should not have problems. If we do it indicates we are incompetent.

15 There is only one way of seeing any situation, i.e., the 'True' way.

- Remember the last time you felt bad about something – angry, jealous, resentful, etc. What were you telling yourself? Were any of these 15 beliefs the basis for your self -talk?

- Now, you are going to challenge the destructive self-talk that caused you those difficulties. Fill in the rest of the table for the event you have just thought about. Write down your self-destructive talk in your own words. They may well include condemnation of yourself and be full of what people should or ought to do.

MY SELF-DEFEATING BELIEF
The event:
What I felt:
What I was telling myself:
What it made me do:
What my self-defeating belief was:

- Now challenge that self-talk, re -interpret it by exchanging the shoulds and oughts for preferences. Talk to yourself about what you can learn from the experience. Tell yourself that you can behave differently next time.

- Fill in the table below with alternative constructive self-talk and the consequences that could have resulted:

Constructive self-talk
Feelings would be
What my self-defeating belief was:

If we can:

1. avoid self-defeating thinking when difficulties arise;

2. develop ways of thinking (using self-talk) based on a more rational approach in time of difficulty;

we will be more likely to manage ourselves and the situation more effectively when things do not turn out as we would wish.

'Men feel disturbed not by things, but by the views which they take of them.'
Epictetus, 1 st Century AD

There may be times when self-defeating talk becomes almost obsessional: you can't get such thoughts out of your mind. Here you have to try something that might sound silly but works – tell yourself firmly to 'Stop!' whenever you catch yourself doing it. Don't make it worse by saying to yourself 'You are stupid to think like that'. That's just more self-defeating talk. Just 'Stop!' and then move on to positive self-talk. Have some positive thoughts or pictures ready to put into your head automatically.

You can work steadily towards giving up all your self-defeating beliefs.

When you are under extra stress, you may find that your favourites – usually the ones that allow you to say rotten things to yourself about yourself – creep back into your mind. This could be a sign to you that you need to pay more attention to looking after yourself under stress.

4 . Looking after yourself under stress.

Research has consistently shown that the fitter we are the more energy we have to cope with the problems that arise and disappointments that are inevitable in everyday life. Keeping fit will help us to prevent undue stress when things do not go well for us. Also when we do experience the ill effects of stress, physical exercise can help us to feel better.

We can dissipate stress through a fitness programme, dancing, sex – all together if we're creative!

The other side to looking after ourselves physically is to learn to relax when all about us is movement, turmoil, frustration, and disappointment. There are many ways of relaxing and perhaps it appears strange to read of this as a skill.

The time to relax is when you don't have time for it!

We would certainly not wish to prescribe to people how they should relax, but it is important for everyone to discover the techniques that work for them. Set out on the next page are some techniques for relaxation.

Techniques which work directly on our bodies

- meditation
- progressive relaxation
- deep breathing
- yoga
- massage

Techniques which work indirectly through a psychological process

- listening to music
- reading a book, watching TV
- having a drink
- going to a peaceful place
- being with people we can be ourselves with

Stimulation as a way of relaxation

Sometimes when we feel tired, we often do not feel like doing anything. Hard work can make us tired so that we physically need a rest. However, when high stress makes us feel tired, a change to a stimulating activity can make us feel better and full of energy again. It helps to think about what is behind our tiredness. You could try the effect of:

- a brisk walk
- a quick shower rather than a relaxing soak in the bath
- dancing
- phoning a friend
- making a snap decision to go out somewhere (meal, film, bowling, bingo, roller skating – something different!).

Which of the options in this list have you tried?

Did they work for you?

Which others might you try?

Keep a record

- Your list of self-defeating beliefs, and what you can do to counter these

---

Exercise 40: Do I know how to look after myself under stress?

RAINBOW BUILDING SKILL: Looking after yourself

When our plans (even the half-conscious ones) do not work out, we can easily feel under a considerable amount of stress as a result. Below are listed a variety of questions about 'Looking after yourself' in stressful situations.

Tick the statements to which you can answer 'yes'.

- ☐ Do I get regular exercise, or have a personal fitness programme?
- ☐ Do I eat regularly and have a balanced diet?
- ☐ Do I keep to a regular schedule?
- ☐ Do I know how to say 'no' to things I don't want, and conversely, do I know how to ask for what I do want?
- ☐ Do I give myself a break, or some kind of a 'treat' when under stress?
- ☐ Do I have people to whom I can turn for help? Do I actually turn to them?
- ☐ Do I know how to relax?
- ☐ Do I talk constructively to myself?

If you scored 7-8, you should be able to cope well with disappointment.

If you scored 4-6, you can cope with some disappointment but would benefit by developing your 'Looking after yourself' skills.

If you scored 0-3, you could be knocked back by disappointment unless you make definite plans to acquire better 'Looking after yourself' skills.

Space does not permit us to discuss each of these issues here. Instead, look at the resources section on page 147 which refers to a number of available materials which are broadly concerned with 'looking after yourself'. Most of these should be available in your local library, or at least they could obtain copies for you. In addition to books, you could enrol in classes on 'Looking after yourself', or yoga, meditation, relaxation, massage, assertiveness, fitness, and time management. Your local library, newspaper, Citizens Advice Bureau, Adult Education Centre, College of Further Education or leisure centre are good places to find out what is going on in your area.

Looking For Ways Forward

When we have coped effectively with our feelings of disappointment, we are free to use our skills of RATIONAL THINKING to help work out what to do next.

If things do not work out as you wish:

1. Reappraise your action plan.

2. If that does not work, reappraise your original objectives.

3. Ask why it didn't work – what was due to your influence, and what was due to external influences?

4. Ask yourself what you can learn from the experience.

5. Always have a back-up plan (Plan B). Develop it alongside Plan A and try to identify check points during Plan A at which you can review progress and if necessary cut your losses and switch to Plan B. Your original plan should be flexible enough for you to be able to revise and improve it as you go along and to enable you to switch to Plan B if need be.

   By all means put everything you've got in to achieving Plan A but don't let the chance to reach your goal fall through because you haven't taken the time to consider other ways of reaching it.

6. Take a lateral step. Consider a different goal if your first choice proves unobtainable.

Whenever you are in a situation that you wish to change there are always four basic strategies for managing that situation illustrated in the figure below.

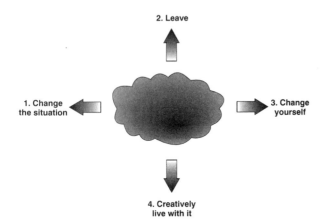

Strategy 1: Change the situation

The first strategy is often that of trying to change the situation to make it more like you want it to be. However, having tried to make changes to no avail, you are left with the other three options.

Strategy 2: Leave

You exit from the situation, job, relationship or problem.

Strategy 3: Change yourself

Perhaps if you changed your ambitions, attitude, behaviour, lifestyle etc, your situation would improve.

Strategy 4: Creatively live with it

This means much more than simply, 'putting up with it'. It requires a conscious strategy so that you can minimise the undesirable aspects of the situation and maximise the desirable ones. Examples might include investing more energy in activities outside your job (if dissatisfied at work), isolating yourself in a project in such a way that it reduces your contact with troublesome elements, or spending more time doing the things you enjoy and cutting down on the others.

Below is an example worked out by someone who was extremely dissatisfied with her job.

CHANGE THE SITUATION	LEAVE
Options • suggest a new project • negotiate for a re-definition of my job • suggest that meetings are more • ask for salary • arrange to work more with people I like	Options • get new job • get leave of absence • get industrial sabbatical • take early retirement • get transfer to another site
CHANGE YOURSELF	**LIVING WITH IT**
Options • lower my expectations • get retrained • undertake in-service training	Options • focus more on other areas of my life • go part-time • take a second job • take an Open University course

We have felt it necessary in this section to prepare you for the worst. Things won't always work out, you will make mistakes, others will block your goals. The challenge for you is how well you react to that?

Will you learn from the experience or disappear into the swamp underneath it?

Rainbow Building Summary Sheet

WHAT IF IT DOESN'T WORK OUT?

1 List the techniques you use to deal with disappointment. Add new ones you are going to try.

Physical: _____

_____

_____

_____

Psychological: _____

_____

_____

_____

List the key people in your support network: _____

_____

_____

_____

_____

2 Which 'looking after yourself' skills do you need to improve or acquire? What are the next steps you have to take in order to do this?

a _____   a _____

b _____   b _____

c _____   c _____

3 List your most common self-defeating beliefs. Translate each of them into more positive self-talk.

a _____   a _____

b _____   b _____

c _____   c _____

AT THE END OF YOUR RAINBOW

ROUTE MAP

for "The end of your rainbow"

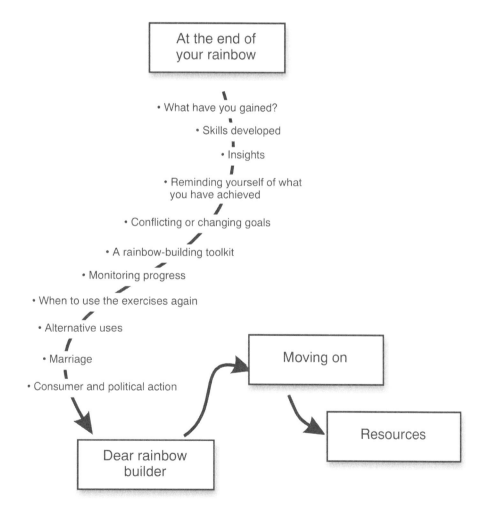

At the end of
your rainbow

- What have you gained?
- Skills developed
- Insights
- Reminding yourself of what you have achieved
- Conflicting or changing goals
- A rainbow-building toolkit
- Monitoring progress
- When to use the exercises again
- Alternative uses
- Marriage
- Consumer and political action

Dear rainbow builder

Moving on

Resources

We have reached the end of our RAINBOW BUILDING programme. How useful has it been for you? This book offers you the chance to find out about yourself. It can tell you how to do it but only you can do the hard work involved. Return to the contract you made with us on page 22. How well have you stuck to the contract?

In part 4 of the contract you were asked to identify ways you have sabotaged yourself in the past. Did you catch yourself doing it this time? Are you now more aware of the ways in which you do it?

For example did you:

- Skim through the book meaning to come back and actually do the exercises – but didn't?

- Only start reading when you were too tired?

- Never allocate sufficient time to do enough work on it?

- Defeat yourself by negative self-talk and turn every exercise into an opportunity to put yourself down?

- Use any of this above list of devices to avoid acknowledging that it can be quite scary to explore yourself in this way?

We are not in a position to challenge you on this: but we are asking you to challenge yourself.

What have you gained?

You can review what you have achieved by looking through the notes you have made and at the progress checks and summary sheets.

Sum up what has proved most important for you in each of these three areas:

1. Information (facts) I've learned.

....
....
....
....
....
....
....
....
....
....
....
....
....
....
....
....
....
....
....
....
....

2. Skills developed

....
....
....
....
....
....
....
....
....
....
....
....
....
....
....
....

3. Insights I have gained (look through your AHA! Folder)

....
....
....
....
....
....
....
....
....
....
....
....
....
....
....
....
....
....

Skills developed

At the start of this book, we said a rainbow-builder needs to develop seven types of skills (page 13). The whole range has been covered but knowing yourself has been the main focus of the exercise. As a rainbow-builder, you need to have a thorough understanding of your raw materials.

The table opposite sums up which skills the various exercises have been helping you to build.

Which of the exercises have proved most useful for you ? Put a tick in the skills columns on the next page, opposite the exercises to indicate in which way you found each exercise to be helpful.

Now consider:

- Are there some exercises you left out that you would like to go back to?

- Do you wish to repeat some of the exercises?

- Which of the seven skills do you want to build up? 'Moving On', page 143, suggests how you could pursue this.

EXERCISE CHECKLIST							
Exercise Numbers	Knowing yourself	Research skills	Learning from your experience	Communi-cating	Making decisions	Setting objectives making action plans	Looking after yourself
1 Drawing my life line.							
2 How do I spend my time?							
3-9 Clarifying my values.							
10 Finding my transferable skills.							
11 What are my interests?							
12 Choosing where to live.							
13 The ages of me.							
14 What life stages am I at now?							
15-17 What kind of career pattern?							
18 How do others see me?							
19 Analysing my time.							
20 Analysing my satisfaction.							
21 My career and life brain pattern.							
22 My fantasy job/career/life/day.							
23 Complaints into objectives.							
24 This is your life... continued.							
25 Let me introduce myself.							
26 My life roles in the future.							
27 My obituary.							
28 What do I earn, what do I spend, what do I need?							
29 My monkey trap.							
30 Buy me today.							
31 Who do I know?							
32 More of... Less of...							
33 12 steps towards clear objectives.							
34 Force field analysis.							
35 Cost benefit analysis.							
36 My action plan.							
37 A letter to myself.							
38 Who do I have to talk to?							
39 Avoiding self-defeating beliefs.							
40 Do I know how to look after myself under stress?							

Insights

In the future, these may be your most vivid memories of working through this book. Insights are usually gained when we are thinking most deeply about ourselves – it's almost as if we have dredged them up. However, it sometimes seems as if we find them too painful – or challenging, and they sink down again out of sight. We forget the insights we have gained.

You can help prevent this happening and gain most from them by taking each of the key insights you have just listed (page 138) and writing some action notes for them. Will you now be on the alert for certain situations to which you will try to react differently? Do you want to change yourself in any way? Or perhaps acknowledge and accept the person you now see yourself to be?

Reminding yourself of what you have achieved

Working through this book should have proved challenging and stimulating. It may at times have been hard work or painful. It's quite an achievement to have examined your life in this way. You should feel proud of yourself. Praise yourself – it's better than praise from others! You might like to write yourself a post-card noting exactly what you are proud of having done. You could pin it up picture side out where you can see it regularly. It will remind you of what's on the other side.

Conflicting or changing goals ?

The Rainbow Building Summary Sheet you completed at the end of Question 5 may well have identified for you that some of your goals conflict. Or you may realise that pursuing some of your goals would conflict with the goals of those you live or work with. This will probably mean that you need to reconsider the priority you give to the various values you have already looked at. You may also need to move on to consider what your values are for personal relationships and for involvement and responsibilities within the community and society.

You've probably already found that at different times in your life you have chosen or been forced to give priority to different goals. It may well be the same in the future.

Your action plans will need to take this into account. Try making short-term and medium-term action plans:

1. Short-term – What will you achieve during the next six months?

2. Medium-term – What, at this moment, do you hope to achieve during the next five years? If you review this plan every year you will have a rolling five year plan that can be more responsive to the changing priorities you may need to give to your goals.

An additional strategy is to keep an up-dated list of what you hope to achieve before the end of your life. The list will certainly change as the balance of your values shifts at successive life stages: Doing this can spur you on to make life happen, rather than to let life happen to you. With this list there is, however, a danger that you will suddenly flip from thinking, 'There's plenty of time to fit everything in', to, 'Good heavens – time is running out'. If this happens, you'll probably then recognise that it counts as a 'mid-life turning point' and that you should go through this Life Management Review again.

A Rainbow-building tool kit

The skills you have learned are transferable. You can go on building rainbows.

Monitoring progress

You may decide to repeat some of these exercises either regularly or at certain times, especially if major changes are coming up. They can be used as a way of quality control monitoring for your life. Below are some suggestions as to how you might use them.

When to use the exercises again

Exercise	When to use
Exercise 2 How do I spend my time? plus Exercise 19 and 20.	• Regular review: demands and needs will vary. • When you are under pressure. • When you feel increasingly tired. • When you are having trouble meeting new commitments.
Exercises 7, 8 and 9 Values and needs	• At different life stages (see Exercise 14) when priorities are likely to change. • When certain life events challenge your values.
Exercise 10 Transferable skills	• Keep this updated (particularly if you want to keep an up-to-date curriculum vitae, but also as a morale-booster).
Exercise 11 What are my interests?	• Check occasionally – your energies and enthusiasms may vary. • Do it to challenge yourself to try new things and to check if those you are saving up for later in life ever get done.
Exercise 14 Life stages	• Check every five years.
Exercise 17 A dual-career family	• Do this when relevant.
Exercise 18 How do others see you?	• Occasionally – if you begin to suspect that your image of yourself needs adjustment in the light of feedback from other
Exercise 21 My life and career brain pattern	• Use to monitor changes in your 'satisfiers' and 'dissatisfiers'.
Exercise 26 Life roles in the future	• Check in ten years' time to see if you were right!

contd/...

Exercise	When to use
Exercise 31 Who do I know?	• Review and revise – this will alert you to where you are losing contact with parts of your network. Do you want to lose contact? • Are you adding new people?
Exercise 32 More of... less of...	• Monitor progress and make new action plans periodically.
Exercise 37 A letter to myself	• Remember to open it!
Exercise 38 Who do I have to talk to?	• Monitor regularly to see that you do. • Check when under stress since these are the people who can best support you.
Exercise 40 Do I know how to look after myself under stress?	• This needs to be kept up all your life. Six-monthly reviews will help

You could make a note in your diary to check through this list during the last days of December when you are beginning to contemplate a New Year.

Alternative uses

The exercises have been developed to help you look at life and career management but you can adapt them to other issues that you want to examine or projects that you want to plan.

Many of them can be used at transition times when you are facing major changes in your life. You may have chosen to make the change and enjoy doing it but the knock-on effects of the change on the whole of your life and perhaps on to other people's make it a stressful time.

Here are some ideas for just two other areas of life:

Marriage

• Exercises 1 and 24 can be adapted to explore the history and possible future of your marriage/partnership. Both partners should draw their own future life lines and discuss them with one another.

• Exercise 6 'Use of leisure' and Exercise 2 plus Exercises 19 and 20 'Analysing the use of time' may help both partners negotiate new contracts. So will Exercise 32 'More of ... Less of ...'

• Exercise17 'A dual career' needs to be done before marriage as well as at various stages during the marriage.

• Exercise 22 'Fantasy' – think about your fantasy partner and fantasy marriage. What does this tell you about yourself? What would be appropriate for you to share with your partner?

Consumer and political action

• Exercise 23 'Turning complaints into objectives' is probably the starting point.

• Exercise 31 'Who do I know?' When members of a group pool the relevant parts of their networks, supportive and influential people can usually be found.

• Exercise 33 'Twelve steps to clear objectives', Exercise 34 'Force field analysis' and Exercise 36 'My action plan' will help you develop a campaign.

• Exercise 35 'Cost-benefit analysis' can help you see pros and cons of a proposed action or choose between options.

'To go faster, you must slow down.'
John Brummer

Dear Rainbow Builder ...

Before you move on, please accept this award with our congratulations for completing this programme!

With these skills, you will go far!

Rainbow Builder

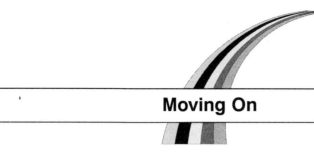
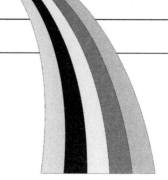

Moving On

The Future

This programme can be hard work. We would suggest that before you move on you relax, take a break, go and have some fun. Then come back and think about your plans for the future. Here are some suggestions you might try.

Your plans might Include:

- seeking out more information;
- building up your life skills;
- gaining more insights into yourself.

Which areas?

Here are a few you might choose from:

- Further work/career management
- Personal relationships
- Looking after yourself
- Leisure interests
- Management skills
- Unpaid work options
- Planning for early retirement.

Resources

Your choice may depend on whether you want to concentrate on information, skills or insights. Consider which of these you might want to use:

Books

In general they are good for information. 'How-to-do-it' books for skills. 'How-to-do-it' human psychology books for insights as well as skills. Ask your library for help in getting relevant book lists.

Counselling/Advice

Ask at the library or Citizens Advice Bureau for what's available in your area.

Consider using career counsellors, marriage counsellors – who accept any life-review concern as a suitable reason for seeking help, or psychotherapy (ask your GP for what is available on the NHS or privately).

Support/Interest groups

These self-help groups may be part of a national network or just a local initiative. The CAB and libraries should know about them. They may be information, support or action focused.

Local classes

You may need direct personal tuition for learning certain skills. Being able to share your experiences with others is an additional benefit. Check local newspapers, libraries and Colleges of Further Education, Adult Education Centres and Community Colleges.

The Internet

There is growing use of the Internet for those with access to the technology, as a means of information gathering, networking and developing support systems. This is an area with a huge future potential for rainbow-builders!

'People travel to wonder at the height of mountains, at the huge waves of the sea, at the long courses of rivers, at the vast compass of the ocean, at the circular motion of the stars; and they pass by themselves without wondering.'

St Augustine

REFERENCES

1. Hopson, B. and Scally, M., *Lifeskills Teaching*, Maidenhead, McGraw Hill,1981.

2. Hopson, B. and Scally, M., *Rainbows, A Teaching Programme for Career and Life Management,* Sheffield, COIC, 1991.

3. Sheehy, G., *Pathfinders*, London, Sidgwick and Jackson,1983.

4. Figler, H., *The Complete Job Search Handbook*, New York, Holt Rinehart Winston,1979.

5. James, Clive, *Unreliable Memoirs*, London, Picador,1981.

6. Campbell, D., *If You Don't Know Where You're Going, You'll Probably End Up Somewhere Else*, Niles, Illinois, Argus,1974.

7. Kelly, E. L., 'Consistency of the adult personality', American Psychologist, 1955, 10, 654-681.

8. Holland, J. L., *Making Vocational Choices: A Theory of Careers*, Prentice-Hall,1973.

9. Levinson, D. J., Darrow, C. N., Klein, E. B., Levinson, M. H. and McKee, B., *The Seasons of a Man's Life*, New York, Alfred Knopf,1978.

10. Neugarten, B. L,. 'Adaptation and the life cycle', in N. K. Schlossberg and A. D. Entine (Eds), *Counselling Adults*, Monterey, California, Brooks/Cole,1977.

11. Hopson, B. and Scally, M., 'Changes and development in adult life: implications for helpers', British Journal of Guidance and Counselling, 1980, 8; 2.

12. Sperry, L., Mickleson, D. J., Hunsaker, P. L., *You Can Make It Happen*, Reading, Mass., Addison-Wesley,1977.

13. Loughary, J., and Ripley, T., *This Isn't Quite What I Had In Mind*, Eugene, Oregon, United Learning,1974.

Resources

BOOKS AND MATERIALS

FOR CAREER AND LIFE MANAGEMENT

What Colour is Your Parachute? - a Practical Manual for Job Hunters and Career Changers Richard Bolles, Richard Nelson, 1999. This is a UK edition of the best-selling US guide to self analysis and "proactive" job hunting. The British supplement primarily consists of books and addresses and the US text is reproduced in its entirety. This makes the information component of the book less relevant to the UK which is a pity because the system is well-tried.

The Chance to Live More Than Once, Barry Curnow and John McLean Fox, Management Books 2000, 1997. A guide to career and life development for 'Third Agers' as they move towards retirement from their main career.

Changing Course: A Positive Approach to a New Job and Lifestyle, Maggie Smith, Management Books 2000, 1992. Shows how people can use the experience of early retirement as an opportunity to review their lives, learn to manage change, develop new interests, relationships and lines of work.

Kaizen and You, Igor Popovich, Management Books 2000, 1997. The book provides a step-by-step approach to implementing a programme for continuous self-improvement – the Japanese art of kaizen.

Lifeskills Personal Development Series, Barrie Hopson & Mike Scally, Management Books 2000, 1991-9. 7 booklets in an easy to use, open-learning format. Suitable for both individual and group use. Topics covered: Transitions; Communication; Assertiveness; Time Management; Relationships; Stress, Health & Your Lifestyle; Learn to Learn.

Super Job Search, Peter K. Studner. Management Books 2000, 1996

FOR LIVING IN THE INFORMATION ERA

The Third Wave, Alvin Toffler, Pan, 1981. Crucial for an understanding of how the Information Era is fundamentally different from the Industrial Era. Very American. Very stimulating, with a global perspective.

The Aquarian Conspiracy: Personal and Social Transformation in the 1980's. Marilyn Ferguson, JP Tarcher, 1987. A wide-ranging account of a unique change in values and relationships identified by the author as happening throughout the world.

Megatrends 2000, John Naisbitt, Avon, 1991. The trends for the Information Era identified by a fascinating technique of trend analysis through local newspapers.

The Age of Unreason, Charles Handy, Arrow, 1995. A vision of an era of new discoveries, new enlightenment and new freedoms. An examination of the concept of discontinuous change and how it can be turned to advantage.

The New Realities, Peter Drucker, Butterworth-Heinemann, 1994. A changing analysis of the information-based organisation, the input of knowledge workers on organisations and the economy, and much more.

FOR ADULTHOOD AND SELF-DEVELOPMENT

New Passages, Gail Sheehy, HarperCollins, 1997. Best seller which charts the progress of adults through all the key life stages. Fascinating case studies enable you to play "spot yourself".

FOR WOMEN

Women in Transition: A Course of Exercises to Help You Get Your Life in Shape, Sara Clay, Management Books 2000, 1992

The Competitive Woman, Janet Cameron, Management Books 2000, 1990. A survival guide for the woman who aims to be boss.

Returning to Work, Women's Returners Network, 1997

Projecting Your Image, Pat Roberts, Management Books 2000, 1991. A practical guide to styling for success.

FOR CAREERS INFORMATION

Part-Time Work, Judith Humphries, Kogan Page, 1986. A guide to your rights, opportunities and conditions of work and all the practical aspect of working part-time.

Occupations, COIC. Published annually. A guide to occupations in the professions, industry, commerce and the public services.

FOR EDUCATIONAL AND TRAINING INFORMATION

Directory of Further Education. The Comprehensive Guide to Courses in UK Polytechnics and Colleges. James Tomlinson and David Weigall (Eds.), CRAC, Hobsons Press, Annually. This really is comprehensive – although it gives little detailed course information. It contains courses at all levels and in almost every academic or vocational area in maintained institutions outside universities Particularly useful for non-advanced further education.

The Natwest Student Book 2000: An Applicant's Guide to UK Colleges, Polytechnics and Universities. K. H. Boehm and J. Lees Spalding (Eds.), Trotman, 1999. Annually. Contains information on places where you can study for a degree. Includes a description of each institution and the main subjects on offer.

Compendium of Advanced Courses in Colleges of Further and Higher Education, Ed. R Eberhard, London and South-Eastern Regional Advisory Council For Further Education. Annually. Very comprehensive summary of all post 'A' Level (and equivalent) courses in maintained institutions outside universities.

Which Degree? Trotman. Published biannually in June. Four volumes covering a range of related disciplines, including one which describes institutions and their facilities. Offers comprehensive, reliable summaries of the content of degree courses. A series of "composite mini prospectuses" for all institutions offering degree level work, grouped according to discipline.

Degree Course Guides, CRAC, Hobsons Press. Updated biannually. Each booklet covers one discipline or closely related disciplines and is revised every second year. Useful framework for choice of degree courses in all British institutions with helpful, comparative information on differences in content and emphasis, teaching methods, entrance requirements, etc.

The Directory of Graduate Studies, CRAC, Hobsons Press, Annual Directory of all postgraduate courses. Comprehensive – unlike some "commercial" directories.

British Qualifications (21st edition), Ed Priestley, Kogan Page, 1991. Comprehensive list of all academic education, technical and professional qualifications including index of abbreviations and designatory letters.

Degree Course Offers, Brian W. Heap, Careers Consultants. *PCAS Handbook*, Trotman. Published annually by the Polytechnics Admissions System. P.O. Box 67, Cheltenham, Glos., GL50 IHY.

UCCA Handbook, Published annually. Universities Central Council on Admissions, P.O. Box 28, Cheltenham, Glos., GL50 1HY.

Choosing Your Degree Course and University, Brian W. Heap (Ed.), Trotman, 1998.

Second Chances: Guide to Adult Education and Training Opportunities, COIC. An annual guide to adult education and training opportunities. Excellent.

The Open Learning Directory, Butterworth-Heinemann, 1997. A guide to the range of open learning available today.

Part-Time Degrees, Diplomas & Certificates, Malcolm Tight, CRAC. This book covers part-time higher education courses at Universities, Polytechnics and Colleges.

FOR TIME OUT

A Year Off ... A Year On?: A Guide to Jobs, Voluntary Service and Working Holidays During Your Education, Lifetime Books. Useful for students and anybody else who wants to spend up to a year in temporary or voluntary work.

The International Directory of Voluntary Work, Victoria Pybus, Vacation Work, 1997. Covers a wide range of full and part-time, home-based and voluntary opportunities in the UK and overseas.

Taking A Year Off, Val Butcher, Trotman, 1997. An excellent book which helps individuals recognise their particular needs and the best use of their time when taking a year off.

FOR JOBS ABROAD

Working Abroad: The 'Daily Telegraph' Guide to Living and Working Overseas, Godfrey Golzen and Margaret Stewart, 1998.

The Directory of Jobs and Careers Abroad (9th Edition), Jonathan Packer, Petersons, 1997.

Directory of Work & Study in Developing Countries, Toby Milner, Vacation Work, 1997. A reference book which covers employment, voluntary work and study opportunities in the Third World.

FOR JOB SEARCHING

Finding the Right Job, Anne Segall with William Greason, BBC, 1990. This book includes information on all aspects of the job search from writing the initial application form to making the right impression at interview.

The Jobsearch Manual, Linda Aspey, Management Books 2000, 1998. Offers a fresh perspective on the entire process of seeking and finding employment. Techniques and tips that are just as relevant to the school or college leaver as they are for the senior executive seeking a career change.

Super Job Search, Peter K. Studner. Management Books 2000, 1996. An accelerated 7-day programme for advanced jobsearch for executives with a proven and marketable track record.

FOR RETIREMENT

The Chance to Live More Than Once, Barry Curnow and John McLean Fox, Management Books 2000, 1997. A guide to career and life development for 'Third Agers' as they move towards retirement from their main career.

Changing Course: A Positive Approach to a New Job and Lifestyle, Maggie Smith, Management Books 2000, 1992. Shows how people can use the experience of early retirement as an opportunity to review their lives, learn to manage change, develop new interests, relationships and lines of work.

FOR SELF-EMPLOYMENT

Working For Yourself: The 'Daily Telegraph' Guide to Self-Employment. Godfrey Golzen, Kogan Page, 1999. Sound advice, information and case studies.

The 'Daily Telegraph' Guide to Taking Up a Franchise, Colin Barrow and Godfrey Golzen, Kogan Page, 2000.

Just for Starters: A handbook for small-scale business opportunities, A Bollard, Intermediate Technology Publications, 1985. (Also, illustrated paperback). Profiles of 33 industries where small enterprises could be profitable.

Make Money at Home (2nd edition), Gordon Wells, Management Books 2000, 1997

Running Your Own Business (3rd Edition), Robert Leach and John Dore, Management Books 2000, 1998. A comprehensive guide to the legal, financial, practical and personal skills needed to run your own business.

Start Your Own Business, Linden Cole, Management Books 2000, June 2000. A complete guide to starting up a new business.

The 'Which?' Guide to Earning Money at Home, Lynn Underwood, Consumers' Association, Hodder, 1996.

The 'Which?' Guide to Starting Your Own Business, Jane Vass, Consumers' Association, 'Which?' Books, 1999

FOR UNEMPLOYED PEOPLE

Job Seeking for Unemployed Graduates. One of AGCAS Information Booklets freely available from most Higher Education careers services.

REFERENCE BOOKS & DIRECTORIES

Reference books and directories are a valuable source of information in job searches. They are usually available in main branches of your Public Library Service, but if you have access to a University or Polytechnic Library, you will also find many specialist reference books not readily available in the local library.

The source directory is:

Current British Directories (CBD)
Lists directories published in the British Isles: "directories which enable a searcher to locate, identify or obtain further information about a person, organisation or other unit; or which provide lists of persons and organisations in a particular industry, trade or group, or in a specific area."

Some of the main reference books are:

Kompass (3 volumes: especially Vol. 2 – Company Information) UK Companies are listed alphabetically and by town within countries. The company information includes key executives, address, telephone number, number of employees and product details. (Further details of products are given in Vol. 1 with financial data in Vol. 1) Volume 1 also includes a list of Trade Associations (by products and services) with the address, telephone number and director or Secretary of those Trade Associations listed.

Key British Enterprises, Dun & Bradstreet Limited, commonly called 'Dun & Bradstreet' (3 volumes):
Volumes 1 & 2
Section 1: Businesses in alphabetical order. Reference volume.
Section 2: Part 1 lists products and services in alphabetical order with the relevant Industrial Classification number. Part 2 lists the Industrial Classification codings with brief description of the trade covered.
Section 3: Gives the names of the businesses under each Industrial Classification.
Section 4: Enables the reader to identify those businesses in a particular classification in a chosen county.

Kelly's Business Directory
Classified list of manufacturers, merchants, wholesalers and firms offering services to commerce and industry (Kelly's also have a number of specialised directories, eg, Oil & Gas Industry).

Directory of British Associations
Lists trade associations, scientific and technical societies, research organisations, chambers of trade, agricultural societies, trade unions, cultural, sports and welfare organisations in the UK and Republic of Ireland. Gives name, address, telephone number and name of Hon. Secretary, Director or Director General.

Directory of Management Consultants in the UK
Full listing of firms offering business consultancy services giving specialisation, industry and geographical area.

British Consultants Bureau Directory
Gives details of all member firms, covering range of experience, expertise and disciplines.

Who Owns Whom (2 volumes and further 2 volumes for Continental Europe) A directory showing links between Parent, Subsidiary and Associate Companies and Membership of Consortium.

Stock Exchange Official Year Book
Turnover, export sales and profits and balance sheets in terms of current cost accounting where published. Each entry includes details of principal subsidiary Companies.

The Times 1000
Annual review of the leading world industrial and financial companies.

Major Companies of – Europe
– The Arab World
Lists name, address and Company with name of directors, principal activities and financial information.

Personnel Manager's Yearbook. Lists recruitment and training organisations and management consultants. Gives name of the individual responsible for recruitment in 4,500 of the country's largest organisations.

Executive Grapevine
Lists Executive Search firms and recruitment consultants.

Examples of specialist directories:
Bankers, Almanac and Year Book
BRAD, Advertiser and Agency List
Directory of Directors
Hollis Press and Public Relations Annual
Insurance Directory and Year Book
The Retail Directory
various professional institutions' directories eg. accountants, lawyers, architects, quantity surveyors.

WHERE TO CONSULT DIRECTORIES

City Business Library, 55 Basinghall Street, London, EC2V 5BX. (0171-638 8215/6); maintains a substantial stock of British Commonwealth and foreign directories.

The Statistics and Market Intelligence Library, 1 Victoria Street, London, SW1H OET. (0171-215 5444); has the best available collection in London of Commonwealth, foreign and international directories.

The British Library (Science Reference Library), Holborn Branch, 25 Southampton Buildings, London, WC2A 1AW. (0171-405 8721); has good stocks of British and foreign directories in the fields of industry, science and technology.

Holborn Library (London Borough of Camden), 32-38 Theobald's Road, London, WC1X 8PA. (0171-405 2705)

Outside London, all large cities, particularly Birmingham Bristol, Glasgow, Leeds, Liverpool, Manchester, Nottingham and Sheffield have extensive collections of directories.

ORGANISATIONS

NETWORKS AND SOURCES OF HELP AND ADVICE FOR LEARNING

Community Education Courses.
Open University Courses exist on Work Choices (based on *Build Your Own Rainbow*), Planned Retirement, Parents and Teenagers, Health Choices, Consumer Decisions, etc. Each course is designed primarily for a specific target group and consists of a short home-study course with text book, audio cassettes, information, accompanying notes and a set of computer marked assignments. Write for details to ASCO, PO Box 76, The Open University, Milton Keynes, MK7 6AA.

Open University.
For details of all their programmes, write to the Open University, Walton Hall, Milton Keynes, MK7 6AA.

LEA Courses
Every LEA has part-time adult education classes. For a prospectus, try your local library, the LEA Offices or the Workers' Educational Association in your area.

University Extra-Mural Classes.
A number of Universities have extra-mural or adult education departments offering courses to the public. Newer ones have continuing education departments. Some Polytechnics and Colleges of Higher Education also have similar facilities.

TV and Radio.
Both the BBC and ITV produce a variety of education programmes, some of them with back-up material. Channel 4 has a special objective of encouraging viewers to learn at home. For information write to:

Educational Liaison Officer, Channel 4 Television, 60 Charlotte Street, London, WIP 2AX
Education Officer (Information), IBA, 70 Brompton Road, London, SW3 1 EY (0171 -584 7011)
Insight Information, BBC, Broadcasting House, London, WIA IAA

For information about educational programmes on the radio write to:

Radio Publicity, BBC, Broadcasting House, London, W1A IAA or telephone 0171-580 4468 ext 2620

The Open College
The Open College is an independent educational charity dedicated to providing flexible training courses to help individuals enhance their vocational skills and improve performance in the workplace. Open College courses cover management and supervisory training, technical and engineering, health care and accountancy, as well as essential vocational skills. Contact the Open College, Freepost TK1006, Brentford, Middlesex, TW8 8BR (0800 300760)

FOR CAREER AND EDUCATION ADVICE AND INFORMATION

Careers Service. Every local education authority has one They are very overstretched in carrying out their statutory responsibilities for young people, but many of them do manage to provide a guidance service for adults. Look in the telephone directory under Careers Service. The service is free.

National Advisory Centre on Careers for Women, 8th Floor, Artillery House, Artillery Row, London, SWIP IRT

Job Centres. This is the first place to ask about all government training opportunities.

TAP (Training Access Point), TAP Employment Department. Information & Advice Services Unit, St Mary's House, c/o Moorfoot, Sheffield, S1 4PO (01742 597344). TAP was set up for the awareness and take-up of work-related education and training opportunities. It offers: detailed information on a wide range of learning opportunities; quick access to information through conveniently located and easy to use terminals; support in putting together a learning programme which meets individual or company needs. Training & Enterprise Councils (TECs) are involved in the contribution TAP can make in meeting the needs of individuals and businesses in their locality.

ECCTIS 2000 (Education Counselling and Credit Transfer Information Services). Oriel House, Oriel Road, Cheltenham, Glos., GL50 1XP. (01242 252627) A computerised database offering a service to students, prospective students and students' advisors, to provide information to help match individual needs to available courses leading to recognised qualifications. This includes information about courses available in a particular area of study together with normal minimum qualifications for entry and, where appropriate, alternative or partial qualifications which have been found to be acceptable

PICKUP Training Directory, Guildford Education Services, 32 Castle Street, Guildford, GU1 3UW (01483 579454). A database of 25,000 entries. It provides information on both public and private sector vocational short courses and other training opportunities. Available on Prestel and MARIS on line, floppy disk, compact disk and annually in print with Macmillan.

Learning Direct, PO Box 900, Manchester, M60 3LL. (0800 100900) National database provides information about where careers advice is obtainable and details of courses and subjects.

Careers Service National Association, 166 Fir Tree Lane, Groby, Leics., LE6 0FH (0116 2870813) A central source of information about locally available careers help and services.

NATIONAL ASSOCIATION OF EDUCATIONAL GUIDANCE FOR ADULTS

National Educational Guidance Initiative. Sponsored by the DES and the Training Agency. The initiative remit encompasses five major areas of work: Consultancy to Local Bodies; Liaison with National Bodies; Training & Development; Dissemination and Strategic Development. Latest publication: Educational Guidance for Adults 1988-89 (UDACE 1990) presents a national overview of educational guidance activity. With the CNAA, NEGI is exploring the development of guidance in HE institutions. NEGI/UDACE, YHAFHE, Bowling Green Terrace, Leeds, LS11 9SX.

The National Association for Education Guidance for Adults (NAEGA) promotes the delivery of high quality educational guidance for adults. There are over 80 services nationwide offering independent and impartial information, advice and counselling to adults wishing to return to education and training. For a copy of the Directory of Services (price £2), contact Anne Docherty, Secretary, The Mews Cottage, 7 Botanic Crescent Lane, Glasgow, G20 8AA

FOR VOLUNTARY WORK

British Executive Service Overseas, 164 Vauxhall Bridge Road, London,SW1V 2RB (0171 6300644)

Voluntary Service Overseas, 317 Putney Bridge Road, London, SW15 2PN. (0181 780 2266)

Oxfam Voluntary Service Council, 274 Banbury Road, Oxford, OX2 7DZ

National Council for Voluntary Organisations, 8 All Saints Street, London, N1 9RL (0171 7136161)

Central Register of Charities, Charity Commissioners, 57-60 Haymarket, London, SW1 OPZ (0171 210 3000)

GAP Activity Projects Ltd, 44 Queens Road, Reading, Berkshire, RG1 4BB. (0118 9594914)

Community Service Volunteers, 237 Pentonville Road, London, N1 9NJ (0171 -278 6601)

International Voluntary Service, Castlehill House, 21 Otley Road, Leeds, L3 3AA (01132 304600)

London Voluntary Service Council, 356 Holloway Road, London, N7 6PA (0171 700 8107)

FOR ALTERNATIVE WORK PATTERNS

New Ways to Work, 309 Upper Street, London N1 OPD (ring 0171-226 4026 between 10 am and 1 pm Tues, Wed and Fri) This produces leaflets on job-sharing and can put you in touch with job-sharing groups around the country.

Industrial Common Ownership Movement, Vassalli House, 20 Central Road, Leeds, LS1 6DE (0113 2461737) Advice and information on how to set up and run worker co-operatives.

Part-Time Careers Ltd, 10 Golden Square, London, W1R 2AF (0171-437 3103)

FOR SELF-EMPLOYMENT

Small Firms Centres (Freephone 2444) will put you in touch with local initiatives to help people thinking of setting up their own businesses. They also provide an initial free consultation service.

Business in the Community, 44 Baker Street, London, W1M 1DH (0171 224 1600) They will tell you if there are any Enterprise Agencies in your part of the country. Some regional offices also.

Enterprise Allowance Scheme. A scheme to help unemployed people start up their own business. If you are unemployed, you can be paid £40 a week for up to a year while you are starting up. Ask for details at your local Job Centre.

Confederation of British Industry (CBI), Centrepoint, 103 New Oxford Street, London, WCIA IDU (0171-379 7400). Includes Small Firms Council.

Crafts Council, 44a Pentonville Road, London N1 9BY (0171 278 7700)

London Enterprise Agency, Small Business Counselling and Training, 4 Snow Hill, London, ECIA 2BS. (0171-236 3000)

Development Board for Rural Wales, Ladywell House, Newtown, Powys, SY16 1JB. (01686 626965) Promotes the economic and social development of mid-Wales and gives advice to those wanting to set up in business.

National Federation of Self-Employed and Small Businesses Ltd, (Head Office) Whittle Way, Blackpool Business Park, Blackpool, SY4 2FE (01253 336000) (Press and Parliamentary Office) 2 Catherine Place, Westminster, London, SW1E 6HF (0171 233 7900)

Northern Ireland Development Board, Local Enterprise Development Unit, Lamont House, Purdys Lane, Belfast, BT8 (01232 232755) 17 The Diamond, Londonderry, BP48 6BR

Scottish Enterprise, 120 Bothwell Street, Glasgow, G2 7JP (0141 248 2700)

Highlands and Islands Development Board, 20 Bridge Street, Inverness, IV1 1 QR. (01463 234171)

URBED, Enterprise Development, 19 Store Street, LOndon WC1E 7DH (0171 436 8050)

FOR UNEMPLOYED PEOPLE

Unemployed Workers' Centres, TUC Unemployed Workers' Centres, Congress House, Great Russell Street, London, WC1B 3LS. (0171-636 4030) These are to be found around the UK and they offer advice for those unemployed and those facing redundancy.

FOR RETIREMENT

REACH (Retired Executives Action Clearing House), Bear Wharf, 27 Bankside, London, SE1 9ET. (0171-928 0452)

Business in the Community, (see above)

Success After Sixty, at Hays Interselection, 40 Old Bond Street, London, W1 X 3AF. (0171-629 0672) Specifically for people with experience in the insurance industry.

British Executive Service Overseas, (see above)

FOR PEOPLE WITH DISABILITIES

RADAR (Royal Association for Disability and Rehabilitation), 12 City Forum, 250 City Road, London, EC1V 8AB (0171 250 3222) Provides a job search information pack.

Employment Opportunities for People with Disabilities, Head Office, 1 Bank Building. Prince's Street, London, EC2R 8EU (0171-726 4963) They provide counselling and training advice on education and employment, as well as trying to find jobs for disabled people.

Disablement Income Group, 5 Archway Business Centre, 19-23 Wedmore Street, London, N19 4RZ (0171 263 3981) Advice for disabled people.

The Disabled Living Foundation, 380 Harrow Road, London W9 2HU (0171 -289 6111)

Disability Alliance (see local telephone directory) Produce an excellent handbook.

FOR BEREAVEMENT AND LONELINESS

CRUSE (support and advice for the bereaved), Cruse House, Sheen Road, Richmond, Surrey. (0181 332 7227)

Samaritans (see local telephone directory): 10 The Grove, Slough, SL1 1QP (01345 909090)

FOR MOVING HOUSE

National Federation of Housing Associations, 30-32 Southampton Street, London, WC2F 7HF (0171 278 6571)

FOR WOMEN

Business and Professional Women UK Ltd, 23 Ansdell Street, Kensington, London, W8 5BN (0171 938 1729)

FOR RELATIONSHIPS

Relate, (see local telephone directory) 7A Sheep Street, Rugby. Formerly the National Marriage Guidance Council. (01788 565675)

FOR CARERS OF ELDERLY RELATIVES

Age Concern England, Astral House, 1268 London Road, London SW16 4ER (0181 679 8000)

Carers National Association, 20-25 Glasshouse Yard, London, EC1A 4JS (0171 490 8818)

Appendix 1
THE 24
JOB FAMILIES

This appendix describes the 24 Job Families referred to in the section WHO AM I? It provides a list of jobs contained within each family, and a key to the level of qualification likely to be required to attain them. Some jobs appear in more than one Job Family; in these cases a capital letter in brackets appears after the job to indicate the other family where it may be found.

You can match your skills and interests against the jobs set out in this appendix to find out which jobs might best suit you.

The Job Families included in this appendix are divided into six groups as follows:

Category	Job Family	Map Region*	Page
1. Business Sales and Management	A. Marketing and Selling	1	154
	B. Management and Planning	2	154
	C. Retail Sales and Services	1	155
2. Business Operations	D. Administration and Information Management	4	155
	E. Cash Handling, Finance and Accounting	3	156
	F. Office Machine Operation	5	157
	G. Storage, Despatch and Delivery	5	157
3. Technologies and Trades	H. General Services	6	157
	I. Repairing and Servicing Home and Office Equipment	6	158
	J. Growing and Caring for Plants and Animals	6	158
	K. Construction and Maintenance	6	159
	L. Transport Equipment Operation	6	159
	M. Engineering Processing and Other Applied Technologies	7	160
4. Natural, Social and Medical Sciences	N. Natural Sciences and Mathematics	8	161
	O. Medicine and Medical Technologies	12	162
	P. Social Sciences and Legal Services	9	166
5. Arts and Media	Q. Performing Arts	10	163
	R. Literary	11	163
	S. Art and Design	10	164
	T. Popular Entertainment and Professional Sport	12	165
6. Social, Health and Personal Services	U. Education and Social Services	12	165
	V. Nursing and Personal Care	12	166
	W. Catering and Personal Services	3	167
	X. Security and Protective Services	4	167

*(*World of Employment Map, page 60)*

Watch Point

JOB FAMILIES WATCHPOINTS

- Don't forget that it is possible to enter some jobs in all of the Job Families by a number of different routes.

- For some jobs experience can compensate for a lack of formal qualifications.

- It is not always possible to enter jobs even if you do have all the necessary qualifications.

- Jobs with the same title can be found at a number of different levels.

- In all Job Families it is possible to move between levels as well as between jobs.

- Even though a Job Family may be found in a particular region of the World of Employment Map, there could be other skills and interests required for individual occupations within this family. Some jobs appear in more than one Job Family, and are cross-referenced accordingly. The purpose of this approach is to suggest some alternatives that you may not have considered previously and that could have relevance to your skills and interests.

| JOB FAMILY | LEVEL 1
Unskilled and semi-skilled jobs. These usually need no specific educational qualifications. Practical abilities are more important. | LEVEL 2
Skilled practical and clerical jobs. These usually involve greater on-the-job training and may require some passes at GCSE/S grade. | LEVEL 3
Supervisory and middle management technician and some professional occupations come into this category. Occupations in this group usually require at least GCSE/S grade (A-C/1-3) and often A levels/H grade passes. Completion of some further training - often full-time - is usually necessary. | LEVEL 4
Professional and higher management occupations Entry to these occupations usually requires the successful completion of a recognised degree or diploma course or extensive experience and highly developed skills at an equivalent level Postgraduate training is often desirable. |
|---|---|---|---|---|

1. BUSINESS SALES AND MANAGEMENT

JOB FAMILY	LEVEL 1	LEVEL 2	LEVEL 3	LEVEL 4
A Marketing and Selling	Fashion/Photographer's Model (Q)
Telephone Sales Person	Sales Representative
Car Sales Executive
Auctioneer
Insurance Agent
Travel Agency Clerk (D)
Sales Negotiator (Estate Agency)
Publicity Officer
Classified Advertising Sales Agent
Market Research Interviewer
Tourist Information Officer (W)
Fashion/Photographer's Model (Q)
Airline Passenger Service Assistant (D)	Advertisement Manager
Account Executive (Advertising Agency)
Insurance Broker
Marketing Executive
Public Relations Executive (R)
Recruiting Officer (MOD)
Literary Agent (R)
Media Executive
Estate Agent
Advertising Copywriter (R)
Ship & Air Broker (G&E)	Marketing Manager (B)
Senior Editor (Publishing) (R)
Market Research Analyst
Estate Agent
Commodity Broker
Company Sales Manager
Stockbroker (E)
Public Relations Executive (R)
Tourist Information Officer (W)
Market Maker (Stock Exchange) (E)
Ship & Air Broker (G & E)
Money Dealer
B Management and Planning	No jobs available at this level	Appeals Officer (Charity)
Party Agent (Political)
Sheltered Workshop Supervisor
Betting Shop Manager
Work Study Assistant (D)	Box Officer Manager
Housing Manager
Laundry and Dry Cleaning Manager
Work Study Officer
Contract Manager
Training Officer (U)
Purchasing Officer/Buyer
Constituency Agent
Cinema Manager
Betting Shop Manager
Car Sales Manager (C)
Land Agent
Bingo Club Manager
Human Resources Executive
Traffic Manager (L)
Garden Centre Manager (J)
Retail Manager (C)
Leisure Manager
Farm Manager (J)
Funeral Director (U)
Assistant Director (Theatre TV) (Q)
Theatre Manager (Q)
Producer (Radio TV) (Q)
Touring Manager (Entertainment) (T)
Team Manager (Sports & Games) (T)
Trainer (U)	Health Service Manager (D)
Human Resources Manager (U)
Museum/Art Gallery Curator (S)
Local Government Administrator (D)
Company Secretary (E)
Contract Manager
Training Manager (U)
Purchasing Manager
Constituency Agent
Betting Shop Manager
Housing Manager
Town Planner (S)
Higher Executive Officer/Executive Officer (Civil Service) (D)
Diplomatic Service Executive Off icer
Company Registrar
Prison Governor (X)
Chief Fire Officer (X)
Chief constable (X)
Chief Security Officer (Private Undertaking) (X)
Transport Manager (G)
Planning and Development Surveyor (K)
Garden Centre Manager (J)
Farm Manager (J)

Fish Farmer/Manager (J)
Principal Nursing Officer (V)
Community Medical Officer (O)
Chief Executive (Local Authority) (P)
Zoo Manager (J)
Stable Manager (J)
Production Manager (M)
Quarry Manager (M)
Director (Theatre/TV) (O)
Producers (TV/Radio) (Q)
Trainer (Private Sector) (U)
Marketing Manager (A)
Manufacturing Manager (A)
Funeral Director (U)

Buyer (Retail Distribution)
Retail Pharmacist (O)
Retail Manager
Antique Dealer (S)

Librarian (R)
Archivist
Information Officer/Scientist (N)
Executive Secretary
Computer Programmer (N)
Systems Analyst (N)
Higher Executive Officer/Executive Officer (Civil Service) (B)
Health Service Manager (B)
Local Government Administrator (B)
Postal Executive/Executive Officer (E)
Air Traffic Control Officer (L)
Environmental Health Officer (U&H)
Trading Standards Officer (U&H)
Banker - Corporate, Domestic, Merchant & International (E)
Bank Manager (E)
Chartered Accountant (E)
Management Accountant (E)
Public Finance Accountant (E)
Certified Accountant (E)
Building Society Manager (E)

Retail Manager (B)
Car Sales Manager (B)
Antique Dealer (S)
Publican/Bar Manager (W)
Fast Food Manager (W)

Supervisor (General & Clerical Occupations) (E)
Executive Secretary
Executive Officer/Administrative Trainee (Civil Service)
Local Government Administrator (B)
Secretary/Personal Assistant
Computer Programmer (N)
Supervisor (Cash Handling & Financial Occupations) (E)
Organising Secretary (Voluntary Organisation) (U)
Housing Officer (U)
Supervisor (IT) (F)

C Retail Sales and Services

Farm Manager (J)
Retail Assistant
Shelf Filler (Supermarket)
Forecourt Attendant (H)
Car Rental Salesman/woman
Milk Roundsman/woman
Checkout Operator
Trainee Butcher (W)
Floristry Assistant (S)
Waiter/Waitress (W)
Barman/Woman (W)
Counter Service Assistant (W)

Bookseller
Antique Dealer (S)
Musical Instrument Sales
Sales Supervisor
Store Demonstrator
Butcher (W)
Florist (S)
Window Dresser/Display Assistant (S)
Publican/Bar Manager (W)
Beauty Consultant (W)
Hairdresser (S & W)
Air Steward/Stewardess (W)

2. BUSINESS OPERATIONS

D Administrative and Information Management

General Clerk
Messenger (G)
Filing Clerk

Data Processing Clerk
Library Clerk (Automatic Data Records)
Bilingual Secretary (R)
Receptionist
Library Assistant (R)
Farm Manager (I)
Secretary
Legal Secretary (P)
Medical Secretary (V)
Farm Secretary (J)
Administrative Officer/Assistant (Civil Service)
Word Processor Operator
Clerical Worker (Local Government)
Travel Agency Clerk (A)
Airline Passenger Service Assistant (A)
Ward Clerk (V)
Medical Records Clerk (V)
Postal Officer
Payroll Clerk (E)
School Secretary (U)
Court Officer (P)

The distinction by occupational levels is adapted from the classification used in 'Job Ideas', Careers and Occupational Information Centre, 1982; also with reference to Standard Occupational Classification

JOB FAMILY	LEVEL 1 *Unskilled and semi-skilled jobs. These usually need no specific educational qualifications. Practical abilities are more important.*	LEVEL 2 *Skilled practical and clerical jobs. These usually involve greater on-the-job training and may require some passes at GCSE/S grade.*	LEVEL 3 *Supervisory and middle management technician and some professional occupations come into this category. Occupations in this group usually require at least GCSE/S grade (A-C/1-3) and often A levels/H grade passes. Completion of some further training - often full-time - is usually necessary.*	LEVEL 4 *Professional and higher management occupations Entry to these occupations usually requires the successful completion of a recognised degree or diploma course or extensive experience and highly developed skills at an equivalent level Postgraduate training is often desirable.*
D Administrative and Information Management (contd)		Justices' Clerks Assistant (P) Accounts Clerk (E) Hotel Receptionist (W) Bank Clerk (E) Audit Clerk (E) Book-Keeper Cost Clerk (E) Sales & Statistics Clerk (E) Invoice Clerk (E) Building Society Clerk (E) Sales Ledger Clerk (E) Tax Officer (E) Postal Officer (E) Air Traffic Control Assistant (L) Insurance Clerk (E) Work Study Assistant (B)		Patent Agent (H) Economist (N) Health & Safety Manager/ Inspector (U&H)
E Cash Handling, Finance and Accounting	Cashier/Rent Collector Coin Collector (Meters) Fee Collector Credit Club Agent	Accounts Clerk (D) Payroll Clerk (D) Bank Clerk (D) Audit Clerk (D) Book Keeper (D) Cost Clerk (D) Sales Statistics Clerk (D) Invoice Clerk (D) Building Society Clerk (D) Tax Officer (D) Accounting Technician Sales Ledger Clerk (D) Postal Officer (D) Insurance Salesman/woman Insurance Clerk (D)	Supervisor (General & Clerical Occupations) (D) Supervisor (Cash Handling & Financial Occupations) (D) Foreign Exchange Clerk (Banking) Securities Clerk Stockbroker's Clerk (A) Pensions Information Officer Rent Officer Accounting Technician Payroll Manager Financial Accountant Claims Official (Insurance) Insurance Surveyor Loss Adjuster (Insurance) Ship & Air Broker (A&G)	Banker Corporate, Domestic, Merchant & International (D) Bank Manager (D) Actuary Licensed Broker (Securities) Investment Analyst (Stock Exchange) Company Registrar Registrar of Stocks and Bonds Tax Consultant Tax Inspector Chartered Accountant (D) Management Accountant (D) Public Finance Accountant (D) Certified Accountant (D) Stockbroker (A) Postal Executive/Executive Officer (D) Building Society Manager (D) Insurance Underwriter Insurance Broker Market Maker (Stock Exchange) (A) Pensions Broker Pensions Consultant Auditor Company Secretary (B) Ship & Air Broker (G&A)

F Office Machine Operation	Reprographic Technician	Supervisor (IT) (D)	
	Reprographic Technician Typist/Word Processor Operator Computer Operator (Data Processing) Telephonist/Receptionist		
G Storage, Despatch and Delivery	Postman/Woman Messenger (D) Store Keeper Warehouse Worker Motor Cycle Messenger Van Driver Furniture Remover	Import Clerk Stock Controller Chartering Clerk (Air Bookings) Load Planner Export Clerk Freight Forwarder Postroom Clerk Shipping Clerk Heavy Goods Vehicle Driver	Ship and Air Broker (E&A) Transport Manager (B) Wholesale Distribution Manager Cash & Carry Manager	Transport Manager (B)er (B) Ship and Air Broker (E&A)

3. TECHNOLOGIES AND TRADES

H General Services	Refuse Collector Removal Worker Window Cleaner Satellite Dish/Television Aerial Erector Car Park Attendant Meter Reader Road Sweeper Ticket Collector Lavatory Attendant Funeral Director's Assistant Mortuary Attendant Laundry Worker Dry Cleaning Assistant Pest Control Officer Bill Poster Porter/Hotel Porter (W) Caretaker (W) Domestic Cleaner (W) Chimney Sweep (W) Window Cleaner (W) Sleeping Car Attendant (W) Lift Attendant (W)	Appliance Demonstrator Patrol (AA/RAC) Picture Framer Wig Maker (S) Document Repairer Driving Instructor Undertaker/Embalmer Assistant Superintendent (Cemetery/Crematorium) Taxidermist Carpet Fitter Lino Fitter Dressmaker (S) Tailor-Bespoke (S) Technical Assistant (Environmental Health Office) Saddler Piano Tuner Pawnbroker Forecourt Attendant (C)	Meat Inspector Kitchen Planner Driving Examiner	Patent Agent (D) Health and Safety Inspector (U&D) Environmental Health Officer (U&D) Trading Standards Officer (U&D)

The distinction by occupational levels is adapted from the classification used in 'Job Ideas', Careers and Occupational Information Centre, 1982; also with reference to Standard Occupational Classification

JOB FAMILY	LEVEL 1 Unskilled and semi-skilled jobs. These usually need no specific educational qualifications. Practical abilities are more important.	LEVEL 2 Skilled practical and clerical jobs. These usually involve greater on-the-job training and may require some passes at GCSE/S grade.	LEVEL 3 Supervisory and middle management technician and some professional occupations come into this category. Occupations in this group usually require at least GCSE/S grade (A-C/1-3) and often A levels/H grade passes. Completion of some further training - often full-time - is usually necessary.	LEVEL 4 Professional and higher management occupations Entry to these occupations usually requires the successful completion of a recognised degree or diploma course or extensive experience and highly developed skills at an equivalent level Postgraduate training is often desirable.
I Repairing and Servicing Home and Office Equipment	Domestic Appliance Service Technician Camera Repairer	Piano Repairer Refrigeration and Air Conditioning Service Mechanic Watch and Clock Repairer Fire/Burglar Alarm Engineer Sewing Machine Engineer Antique Furniture Repairer (S) Musical Instrument Repairer Upholsterer (S) Installation and Maintenance Engineers for: Computers, Photocopiers, Franking Machines, Cash Registers, Postage Machines Domestic Appliance Service Engineers TV/Video and Radio Engineers Computer Service Engineer Telephone Technician Telecommunications Technician	Telephone Technician Telephone Engineer Computer Service Engineer	
J Growing and Caring for Plants and Animals	Horticultural Worker Kennel Hand Stable Hand (T) Agricultural Worker Orchard Worker Turf Layer Agricultural Machinery Operator Forest Worker Tree Feller Hedger Crop Harvester Groom Groundsman/Woman Dog Beautician	Veterinary Nurse Animal Technician Farrier Zoo Keeper Pigman/woman Poultryhand Gamekeeper Beekeeper Gardener Stockman/woman Agricultural Mechanic (M) Tree Surgeon Foreman/woman (Mixed Farming Workers) Nurseryman/woman Guide Dog Trainer Dog Beautician Fish Farm Technician Water Keeper Groundsman/woman Farm Secretary (D)	Foreman/woman (Mixed Farming Workers) Arboriculturist Farm Manager (B) RSPCA/SPCA Inspector Fish Farmer Countryside Rangers and Wardens Forester Mobility Instructor (Guide Dogs for the Blind) (U) Water Bailiff Riding Instructor Market Garden Manager (B) Garden Centre Manager Stable Manager	Botanist (N) Veterinary Surgeon (N) Zoologist (N) Farm Manager (B) Forest Officer/Forestry Manager Horticultural Manager (B) Scientific Officer (N) Landscape Architect (S) Market Garden Manager (B) Ecologist (N) Biologist (N) Zoo Manager (B) Fish Farmer/Manager (B) Ornithologist (N) Marine Biologist (N) Stable Manager (B) Soil Scientist (N)

Jockey/Equestrian Rider (T)
Golf Green Keeper (T)
Riding Instructor (U&T)
Arboriculturist
Dog Handler (X)

K Construction and Maintenance

Cleaning Contract Worker	Electrician	Planning Technician	Structural Engineer (N)
Builders Labourer	Stonemason	Site Manager (Construction)	Civil Engineer (N)
Demolition Worker	Painter and Decorator	Boat Builder	Architect (S)
Fireplace Builder	Plumber	Building Technician	Surveyor - Quantity/Land/
Floor and Wall Tiler	Plasterer	Civil Engineering Technician	Hydrographic Surveyor (N)
Roofing Felt Fixer	Boat Builder	Architectural Technician (S)	Surveyor Building (N)
Fence Erector	Cabinet Maker	Surveying Technician	Planning/Development Surveyor (B)
Mastic Asphalt Spreader	Construction Plant Fitter		
Composition Floor Layer	Contractors Plant Repair &		
Sewer Worker	Maintenance Fitter		
Tile Layer	Heating and Ventilating Fitter		
Caretaker	Scaffolder		
Construction - Labourer/Gang	Roofer		
Worker	Slater/Tiler		
	Paver		
	Monumental Mason		
	Steeplejack		
	Auto-Electrician		
	Technical Assistant (Housing-Local		
	Govt.)		
	Gas Fitter		
	Wrought-Iron Smith (S)		
	Bricklayer		
	Carpenter & Joiner		
	Glazier		
	Thatcher		
	Shop Fitter		
	Stage Carpenter (Q)		

L Transport Equipment Operation

Deck and Harbour Worker	Train Driver	Air Traffic Engineer	Airline Pilot
Lock Gate Keeper	Engine Room Rating (Merchant	Flight Engineer	Test Pilot
Seaman/woman	Navy)	Merchant Navy Deck Officer	Flying Instructor (U)
Drivers' Mate	Lighthouse Keeper	Traffic Assistant (Railways)	Flight Navigator
Deckhand	Air Traffic Control Assistant (D)	Traffic Manager (B)	Pilot (Ship)
Chauffeur	Survey Sounder	Dock Foreman/woman	Master (Foreign-Going Ship)
Rail Service Conductor	Shunter (Railways)	Foreman/woman (Marshalling Yard -	Helicopter Pilot
	Aircraft Refueller	Railways)	Hovercraft Pilot
	Signal Operator (Railways)	Movements Inspector	Air Traffic Control Officer (D)
	Heavy Goods Vehicle Driver	Foreman/Woman (Earth-moving and	
	Bus/Coach Driver	Civil Engineering Equipment	
	Taxi Driver	Operating Occupations)	
	Coast Guard (X)	Port Control Signalman/woman	
	Fireman/woman (X)	Merchant Navy Engineering	
		Officer (M)	
		Merchant Navy Radio Officer	

The distinction by occupational levels is adapted from the classification used in 'Job Ideas', Careers and Occupational Information Centre, 1982; also with reference to Standard Occupational Classification

JOB FAMILY	LEVEL 1	LEVEL 2	LEVEL 3	LEVEL 4
	Unskilled and semi-skilled jobs. These usually need no specific educational qualifications. Practical abilities are more important.	*Skilled practical and clerical jobs. These usually involve greater on-the-job training and may require some passes at GCSE/S grade.*	*Supervisory and middle management technician and some professional occupations come into this category. Occupations in this group usually require at least GCSE/S grade (A-C/1-3) and often A levels/H grade passes. Completion of some further training - often full-time - is usually necessary.*	*Professional and higher management occupations Entry to these occupations usually requires the successful completion of a recognised degree or diploma course or extensive experience and highly developed skills at an equivalent level Postgraduate training is often desirable.*
M Engineering Processing & Other Applied Technologies	Machine Tool Operator	Aircraft Maintenance Engineer	Supervisor in Making and Repairing Occupations eg: glassworking, clay and stoneworking, printing and photographic processing, book binding, paperworking, paperboard products, textile materials, leather working, rubber and plastics, metal and electrical products and related coating operations.	Control Engineer
	Packer	Automatic Lathe Setter		Drilling Engineer
	Paper Mill Worker	Capstan Setter/Operator		Electrical Engineer
	Clothing Production Worker	Plater		Mechanical Engineer
	Food Packer	Engineering Inspector		Production Engineer
	Garment Examiner	Fitter (Jig and Tool)		Biomedical Engineer (N)
	Sewing Machine Operator	Flight Engineer		Chemical Engineer
	Glass Lathe Worker	Machine Tool Setter	Colliery Official	Quarry Manager (B)
	Brickmaker	Metal Spinner	Reprographic Technician	Naval Architect
	Cine-Film Processing Cutting and Assembling Worker	Die Miller	Signals and Telecommunications Technician	Nuclear Engineer (N)
	Cutter (Garments)	Plate-maker (Printing)	Mining Surveyor	Printing Technologist
	Product Finisher	Precision Grinder	Printing Machine Manager	Textile Technologist
	Warp Spinning Machine Operator	Sheet Metal Worker	Industrial Radiographer	Ceramics Technologist
	Cigarette Making Machine Operator	Textile Weaver	Quality Control Inspector	Colour Technologist
	Band Knife Operator	Wallpaper Printer	Quarry Manager (B)	Food Scientist Technologist (N)
	Woodworking Machinist	Cutting Machinist	Toolpusher (Oil Drilling)	Fuel Technologist
	Electronic Bench Tester	Pneumatics and Hydraulics Fitter	Driller (Oil Drilling)	Glass Technologist
	Assembler	Miner	Derrickman (Oil Drilling)	Leather Technologist
	Chemical Plant Operative	Printer	Production Manager (B)	Packing Technologist
	Tyre/Exhaust Fitter	Engineering Instructor	Technical Author (N&R)	Paint Technologist
	Oil Drilling	Electrical Fitter	Film Cameraman/woman (Q)	Lighting Engineer
	Production Worker	Mining Engineering	Soundman/woman (Film/TV) (Q)	Patent Examiner
	Engineering Machine Operator	Craftsman/woman	Merchant Navy Engineering Officer (L)	Hydrographic Surveyor
		Patternmaker (Foundry)		Brewer
		Quality Control Assistant		Energy Technologist and Environmental Engineer
		Electronic and Circuit Inspector		Computer Engineer
		Carpet Weaver		Ergonomist
		Circular Machine Knitter		Water Engineer
		Optical Slab Grinder and Polisher		Petroleum Engineer
		Glass Cutter (Decorations)		Electronic Engineer
		Plaster Mould Maker (Pottery)		Rubber Technologist
		Electrotyper		Printing Technologist
		Photographic Finisher		Polymer Technologist
		Moulder/Core-Maker (Foundry)		Mining Engineer
		Wood Sawyer, Saw Doctor, Dyer		Broadcasting Engineer
		Printing Machine Manager		Development Engineer
		Fabric Weaver		Oil Drilling Rig Manager/Toolpusher
		Aero-Engine Fitter		Production Manager (B)
		Agricultural Mechanic (J)		Technical Author (N&R)
		Maintenance Fitter		
		Contractors Plant Mechanic		
		Roughneck (Oil Drilling)		

Auto Electrician
Welder
Motor Mechanic
Theatrical Electrician (Q)
Soundman/woman (Film/TV) (Q)
Photographic Technician (S)
Technician - Education (U)

4. NATURAL, SOCIAL AND MEDICAL SCIENCES

N Natural Sciences and Mathematics

Tracer/ Drawing Office Assistant

Laboratory Technician (Educational Laboratories)
Laboratory Technician (Industrial Laboratories)
Cartographer (S)
Ordnance Survey Technician
Draughtsman/woman (S)
Laboratory Assistant
Technicians - Medicine & Medical Technologies (O)

Assistant Scientific Officer (Civil Service)
Ordnance Survey Technician
Statistics Officer
Food Technologist
Technical Author (R&M)
Computer Programmer (D)
Metallurgy Technologist
Laboratory Technician (Educational Laboratories)
Laboratory Technician (Industrial Laboratories)
Technicians - Medicine & Medical Technologies (O)
Radiographer (V)

Biologist (J)
Biophysicist
Geologist
Microbiologist (O)
Scientific Officer (Civil Service) (J)
Chemist
Public Analyst
Astronomer
Mathematician
Metallurgist
Meteorologist
Physicist
Statistician
Forensic Scientist
Taxonomist
Ecologist (J)
Mineralogist
Oceanographer
Archaeologist
Minerals Surveyor
Materials Scientist
Bacteriologist
Biochemist
Scientific Journalist (R)
Systems Analyst (D)
Professional Scientist
Food Scientist (M)
Computer Programmer (D)
Geophysicist
Economist (D)
Information Officer/Scientist (D)
Systems Analyst (D)
Botanist (J)
Veterinary Surgeon (J)
Zoologist (J)
Ornithologist (J)
Marine Biologist (J)
Soil Scientist (J)
Surveyor (K)
Structural Engineer (K)

The distinction by occupational levels is adapted from the classification used in 'Job Ideas', Careers and Occupational Information Centre, 1982; also with reference to Standard Occupational Classification

JOB FAMILY	LEVEL 1 *Unskilled and semi-skilled jobs. These usually need no specific educational qualifications. Practical abilities are more important.*	LEVEL 2 *Skilled practical and clerical jobs. These usually involve greater on-the-job training and may require some passes at GCSE/S grade.*	LEVEL 3 *Supervisory and middle management technician and some professional occupations come into this category. Occupations in this group usually require at least GCSE/S grade (A–C/1-3) and often A levels/H grade passes. Completion of some further training - often full-time - is usually necessary.*	LEVEL 4 *Professional and higher management occupations Entry to these occupations usually requires the successful completion of a recognised degree or diploma course or extensive experience and highly developed skills at an equivalent level Postgraduate training is often desirable.*
N Natural Sciences and Mathematics (contd)				Civil Engineer (K) Nuclear Engineer (M) Biomedical Engineer (M) Technical Author (M&R) Dentist/Dental Surgeon (V) Medical Laboratory Scientist (O) Surgeon (O) Engineers and Technologists
O Medicine and Medical Technologies	Sterile Supplies Worker (Hospital)	Medical Laboratory Technician (N) Medical Physics Technician (N) Physiological Measurement Technician (N) Cardiological Technician (N) Electro-encephalography Technician (N) Contact Lens Technician (N) Audiology Technician (N) Neurophysiology Technician (N) Dispensing Technician (Pharmacy) (N) Dental Technician (N) Medical Photographer (N)	Physiological Measurement Technician (N) Cardiological Technician (N) Electro-encephalography Technician (N) Contact Lens Technician (N) Audiology Technician (N) Neurophysiology Technician (N) Diagnostic and Therapeutic Radiographer Medical Laboratory Technician (N) Medical Physics Technician (N)	Optometrist Ophthalmic Optician Pathologist Pharmacist (Hospital) Pharmacologist Anaesthetist Radiologist Surgeon (N) Hospital Doctor Community Medical Officer (B) General Medical Practitioner Community Health Service Doctor Psychiatrist Orthoptist Retail Pharmacist (C) Medical Laboratory Scientist (N) Homeopathic Doctor/Homeopath Microbiologist (N)
P Social Sciences and Legal Services	Court Usher	Court Officer (D) Justices' Clerks Assistant (D) Barristers' Clerk Legal Secretary (D)	Senior Barristers' Clerk General Secretary (Trade Union) Legal Executive Court Reporter	Psychologist (Child, Clinical, Occupational) (V&U) Historian Political Scientist Sociologist Geographer Criminologist Judge Barrister/Advocate Solicitor Economist (E) Anthropologist

Chief Executive (Local Authority) (B)
Court Clerk
Procurator Fiscal
Crown Prosecutor
Clerk to the Justices
Probation Officers (U)

5. ARTS AND MEDIA

P Performing Arts

Costume Assistant
Wardrobe Assistant (TV)
Dresser (Theatrical)
Cinema Projectionist
Stage Hand
Floor Assistant Broadcasting
Fashion/Photographer's Model (A)

Session Musician
Assistant Stage Manager
Make-up Artist (S)
Stage Carpenter (K)
Film Assembler
Acrobat
Theatrical Electrician (M)
Singer
Musical Instrument Maker
Dancer
Production Assistant
Conjurer
Clown
Choreographer (S)
Actor/Actress
Assistant Floor Manager
Film Cameraman/woman (M)
Soundman/woman (Film/TV) (M)
Fashion/Photographer's Model (A)

Animator (Films)
Session Musician
Assistant Theatre Director
Actor/Actress
Presenter (TV, Radio) (T)
Newsreader (TV, Radio) (T)
Drama Coach
Film Director
Singer
Dancer
Music Teacher (U)
Research (Broadcasting)
Stage Manager
Theatre Manager (B)
Choreographer (S)
Composer
Orchestrator
Arranger
Assistant Director (Theatre/TV) (B)
Casting Director (Film and Theatre) (B)
Film Camera Man/woman (M)
Dance Teacher (U)
Floor/Studio Manager
Soundman/woman (Film TV) (M)
Commentator (T)
Producers/(Radio/TV) (B)
Programme Organiser (TV/Radio) (T)
Newsreader (T)

Orchestral Musician
Director (Theatre) (B)
Film Director
Presenter (Broadcasting)
Arts Administrator
Conductor (Musical)
Choreographer (S)
Session Musician
Composer
Orchestrator
Director (TV) (B)
Casting Director (Film and Theatre) (B)
Producer (TV/Radio) (B)
Art Director (Films) (S)
Commentator (T)
Senior Announcer (Radio/TV) (T)
Programme Organiser (TV/Radio) (T)
Music Therapist (v)
Drama Therapist (v)

R Literary

Novelist
Poet
Scriptwriter

Proof Reader
Greetings Card Editor
Magazine Writer (Freelance)
Library Assistant (D)
Bilingual Secretary (D)
Novelist
Poet
Scriptwriter
Reporters (Radio TV)

Editor Commissioning/Desk (Publishing)
Editor (Newspaper)
Interpreter
Reviewer/Critic - Theatre/ Restaurant/Books etc
Translator
Journalist - Newspaper/Magazine/ Freelance

Reader (Publishing)
Editorial Assistant (Publishing)
Advertising Copywriter (A)
Technical Author (N&M)
Reporter - Local/National Newspaper
Proof Reader
Playwright
Scriptwriter
Public Relations Officer (A)

The distinction by occupational levels is adapted from the classification used in 'Job Ideas', Careers and Occupational Information Centre, 1982; also with reference to Standard Occupational Classification

JOB FAMILY	LEVEL 1	LEVEL 2	LEVEL 3	LEVEL 4
	Unskilled and semi-skilled jobs. These usually need no specific educational qualifications. Practical abilities are more important.	*Skilled practical and clerical jobs. These usually involve greater on-the-job training and may require some passes at GCSE/S grade.*	*Supervisory and middle management technician and some professional occupations come into this category. Occupations in this group usually require at least GCSE/S grade (A–C/1-3) and often A levels/H grade passes. Completion of some further training - often full-time - is usually necessary.*	*Professional and higher management occupations Entry to these occupations usually requires the successful completion of a recognised degree or diploma course or extensive experience and highly developed skills at an equivalent level Postgraduate training is often desirable.*
R Literary (contd)		Sub Editor Ghost Writer Biographer Literary Agent (A) Travel Courier (W) Technical Author	Playwright Scriptwriter Conference Interpreter Linguist (Translator/Interpreter) Senior Editor (Publishing) (A) Editor (Newspaper) Interpreter Translator Journalist Magazine Writer (Freelance) Reporter Librarian (D) Technical Author (N&M)	Public Relations Officer (A) Reporter/(TV/Radio) Sub Editor Ghost Writer Biographer Scientific Journalist (N)
S Art and Design	Floristry Assistant (C) Display Assistant Cake Decorator (W)	Draughtsman/woman (N) Ceramics Painter Embroiderer Jewellery Engraver Industrial Photographer Leather Worker Lighting Designer Paste-up Artist Picture Restorer Pottery Worker Sign Writer Silversmith Window Dresser Stencil/Screen Maker Technician (Sculpture) Wallpaper Designer Etcher, Engraver Bookbinder Photographer Portrait Photographer Photographic Technician (M) Hairdresser (W&C) Sculptor Antique Dealer (C) Florist (C) Window Dresser/Display	Photo Journalist Technical Illustrator Architectural Technician (K) Footwear Designer Clothing Designer Fashion Designer Graphic Designer Press Photographer Portrait Photographer Set Designer (Theatre, Television) Interior Designer Industrial Designer Wallpaper Designer Industrial Photographer Commercial Photographer Photographer Textile Designer Beauty Therapist (V&W) Sculptor Silversmith Antique Dealer (C) Kitchen Planner (H) Choreographer (Q)	Landscape Architect (J) Fine Artist Clothing Designer Fashion Designer Graphic Designer/Illustrator Visualiser (Advertising) Interior Designer Industrial Designer Art Director (Advertising Agency) Art Therapist (V) Art Director (Films) (Q) Architect (K) Photographer Footwear Designer Textile Designer Town Planner (B) Antique Dealer (C) Choreographer (Q) Museum/Art Gallery Curator (B)

Assistant (C)
Antique Furniture Repairer (I)
Make Up Artist (Q)
Choreographer (Q)
Cordon Bleu Chef (W)
Wig Maker (H)
Upholsterer (I)
Tailor Bespoke (H)
Dressmaker (H)
Cartographer (N)
Wrought-iron Smith (K)

Team Manager (Sports and Games) (Q)
Senior Announcer (Radio, TV) (Q)
Sports Instructor, Coach
Commentator (Q)
Programme Organiser (TV/Radio) (Q)
Leisure & Recreation Manager (W)

Puppeteer
Impersonator
Golf Green Keeper (J)
Riding Instructor (J&U)
Comedian
Disc Jockey
Ringmaster
Stuntman/woman
Professional Sportsman/woman:
Team Sports:
Soccer, Cricket, Basketball, Rugby League
Individual Sports:
Golf, Lawn Tennis, Boxing, Darts, Snooker, Wrestling, Cycling, Motorsports, Stuntman/woman, Racing Car Driver.
Equestrian Rider/Jockey (J)
Musician, Singer (Popular Music)

Touring Manager (Entertainment) (B)
Sports Instructor/Coach
Sports Official
Team Manager (Sports and Games) (B)
Announcer (Radio, TV) (Q)
Commentator (Sports and Events) (Q)
Newsreader (Q)
Leisure and Recreation Manager (W)

Cinema/Theatre Attendant
Swimming Pool Attendant
Sports Assistant
Stablehand (J)

T Popular Entertainment and Professional Sport

6. SOCIAL, HEALTH AND PERSONAL SERVICES

U Education and Social Services

Nursery Assistant
Organiser of Clubs for the Disabled
Playgroup Organiser
Home Care Assistant (Social Services)
Warden, Sheltered Accommodation
Care Assistant (Residential & Non-Residential)
Play Leader
Classroom Assistant
Childminder (W)

Day Care Centre Staff
Community Centre Worker
Education Welfare Officer
Play Group Leader
Social Work Assistant
Nursery Nurse
Visiting Officer DHSS
Nanny (W)
School Secretary (D)
Technician Education (M)
Driving Instructor

Organiser (Citizens Advice Bureau)
Organising Secretary (Voluntary Organisation) (D)
Community Development Officer
Community Relations Officer
Home Help Organiser
Community Drama Worker
Private Driving Instructor
Road Safety Officer
Tutor/Organiser WEA
Safety Officer
Adult Education Teacher
Minister of Religion
Housing Officer (D)

Lecturer (University, Polytechnic, College of Further and/or Higher Education)
Teacher (Primary, Secondary, Special Schools)
Organiser (Citizens Advice Bureau)
Education Officer (Museum & Art Galleries)
Community Relations Officer
Educational Psychologist (P)
Careers Officer
Adult Literacy Organiser
Minister of Religion
Medical Social Worker

The distinction by occupational levels is adapted from the classification used in 'Job Ideas', Careers and Occupational Information Centre, 1982; also with reference to Standard Occupational Classification

JOB FAMILY	LEVEL 1 *Unskilled and semi-skilled jobs. These usually need no specific educational qualifications. Practical abilities are more important.*	LEVEL 2 *Skilled practical and clerical jobs. These usually involve greater on-the-job training and may require some passes at GCSE/S grade.*	LEVEL 3 *Supervisory and middle management technician and some professional occupations come into this category. Occupations in this group usually require at least GCSE/S grade (A-C/1-3) and often A levels/H grade passes. Completion of some further training - often full-time - is usually necessary.*	LEVEL 4 *Professional and higher management occupations Entry to these occupations usually requires the successful completion of a recognised degree or diploma course or extensive experience and highly developed skills at an equivalent level Postgraduate training is often desirable.*
U Education and Social Services (contd)			NSPCC/RSSPC Inspector Private Employment Agency Consultant/Interviewer Disablement Resettlement Officer Instructor (Prison Service) Trainer Training Officer (B) Personnel Officer (B) Dance Teacher (Q) Home Economist (W) Mobility Instructor (Guide Dogs for the Blind) (J) Funeral Director (B) Riding Instructor (J&T)	Youth & Community Worker Probation Officer (P) Field Social Worker Residential Social Worker Court Liaison Officer (Social Services) Home Teacher Teacher - Prison Service Trainer Education Administrator Education Advisor Private Employment Agency Consultant/Interviewer Training Manager (B) Personnel Manager (B) Health & Safety Inspector (H&D) Environmental Health Officer (D&H) Trading Standards Officer (H&D) Home Economist (W) Flying Instructor (L) Funeral Director (B)
V Nursing and Personal Care	Ward Orderly Nursing Auxiliary/Assistant Ambulance Driver Hospital Porter Occupational Therapist's Assistant	Dental Hygienist Dental Surgery Assistant Artificial Limb Fitter Ambulanceman/Woman Nurse: Hospital Ward Clerk (D) Medical Records Officer (D) Medical Secretary (D)	Radiographer (N) District and Community Nurse Occupational Health Nurse Nurse: Hospital & Midwife Dental Technician Play Therapist Beauty Therapist (W&S) Health Visitor Speech Therapist Aroma Therapist	Dentist/Dental Surgeon (N) Dietitian Orthoptist Principal Nursing Officer (B) Clinical Psychologist (P) Chiropodist Speech Therapist Health Visitor Physiotherapist Occupational Therapist Dispensing Optician Remedial Gymnast Art Therapist (S) Music Therapist (Q) Drama Therapist (O)

W Catering and Personal Services	Waiter/ress (C) Porter/Hotel Porter (H) Bar Staff (C) Canteen Assistant Kitchen Assistant Holiday Camp Staff Hostel Assistant Hotel Room Attendant Valet Maid Kitchen Porter Sleeping Car Attendant (H) Caretaker (H) Cleaner/Domestic (H) Chimney Sweep (H) Lift Attendant (H) Cloakroom Attendant Mothers' Help Counter Service Assistant (C) Linen Room Attendant (H) Window Cleaner (H) Trainee Butcher (C) Cake Decorator (S) Childminder (U)	Air Steward/Stewardess (C) Cordon Bleu Chef (S) Cook School Meals Supervisor Butler Waiter Chief Steward Head Barman/woman Carver Club Steward/ess Hotel Receptionist (D) Beauty Consultant (C) Hairdresser (C&S) Masseur/se Cosmetic Electrolysist Manicurist Pedicurist Tourist Information Officer (A) Housekeeper Publican/Bar Manager (C) Warden/Hostel Warden Butcher (C) Nanny (U)	Purser Housekeeper Home Service Adviser Leisure and Recreation Manager (T) Hotel Manager Publican/Bar Manager (C) Institutional Manager Home Economist (U) Travel Courier (R) Tourist Information Officer (A) Restaurant/Catering Manager Warden/Hostel warden Beauty Therapist (V8S) Fast Food Manager (C) Head Waiter
			Home Economist (U) Hotel Manager Leisure and Recreation Manager (T) Institutional Manager Restaurant/Catering Manager
X Security and Protective Services	School Crossing Attendant Security Guard Traffic Warden Private Detective Gate Keeper Park Keeper Estate Ranger Member of Armed Forces (Non-Commissioned)	Dog Handler (J) Police Officer Fireman/Woman (L) Dock Policeman/woman Prison Officer Fire Prevention Officer Non-Commissioned Officer Coastguard (L) County Court Bailiff Customs Officer Member of Armed Forces (Non-Commissioned) Security Officer/Guard British Transport Police Private Detective	Assistant Prison Governor Armed Forces, Commissioned Service Non-Commissioned Officer Customs Officer Police Officer Assistant Chief Fire Officer Railway Policeman/woman Airport Policeman/woman Immigration Officer
			Prison Governor (B) Chief Constable (B) Chief Security Officer (Private Undertaking) (B) Chief Fire Officer (B)

The distinction by occupational levels is adapted from the classification used in 'Job Ideas', Careers and Occupational Information Centre, 1982; also with reference to Standard Occupational Classification

This appendix describes the six Occupational Interest Groups referred to in the section WHO AM I? – Practical, Investigative, Artistic, Social, Enterprising and Organisational/Administrative. It provides a representative selection of possible jobs or occupations to suit each group type.

OCCUPATIONAL INTEREST GROUPS

The occupations here include representative examples from a comprehensive range of occupations available in the UK. Based on the 'World of Employment Map', they are classified under the following code letters:

P - Practical
I - Investigative
A - Artistic
S - Social
E - Enterprising
O - Organisational/Administrative

Practical Occupations include skilled trades, technical and some service occupations, which involve physical co-ordination or strength, using and repairing machinery and understanding mechanical principles or exploiting natural resources.

Investigative Occupations include scientific and some technical occupations, which involve an interest in how and why things work or happen, and interest in discovering the facts of a situation, analysing and solving problems.

Artistic Occupations include visual and performing arts; design and literary occupations.

Social Occupations include educational and social welfare; occupations which involve advising, understanding and helping others with their problems.

Enterprising Occupations include managerial, sales, financial and service occupations, which involve an interest in managing, leading, negotiating with others or promoting projects.

Organisational/Administrative Occupations include office and clerical occupations, public administration and security, and involve interest in directing or organising procedures by means of paper work.

The three letter Code provides descriptions of occupations. For example, a Code of ESO for a Sales Manager means sales management offers a lot to people with 'enterprising' interests; something for people with 'Social' interests and a little 'Organisational/Administrative' interest. In this way, the Codes provide a brief summary of what an occupation is like by showing its degrees of resemblance to the three major occupational groups which offer scope for these interests.

> **Watch Point**
>
> - Not every combination of letters has a list of occupations. For example, if you have ISE you will not find a list of occupations. You then look up the Nearest combinations – IES, SIE, EIS.
>
> - Don't worry if the occupations listed under your letters really do not appeal. Ask yourself what it says about your interests, e.g. if car sales does not fit for you, how about computer sales?

Occupation	WEM Refce	Job Family

PRACTICAL OCCUPATIONS

PIA

Motor vehicle body repairer/sprayer	6	I
Document repairer	6	H
Piano repairer	6	I
Wallpaper printer	7	M
Tracer/drawing office assistant	8	N
Cartographic draughtsperson	8	N
Planning technician (construction)	6	K
Stagehand	10	Q
Shopfitter	1	C
Theatrical electrician	10	Q
Stage carpenter	10	Q
Architectural technician	10	S
Bookbinder	10	S
Stencil/screen maker	10	S
Photographic technician	8	N

PIS

Beauty Therapist	3	W
Cosmetic electrolysist	3	W
Dental hygienist	12	V
Remedial gymnast	12	V
Home economist	3	W
Radio and TV servicing	6	I
Animal nurse	6	J

PIE

Band knife operator	7	M
Printer	7	M
Chemical plant operative	7	M
Tree surgeon	6	J
Machine tool operator	7	M
Agricultural mechanic	7	M
Boat builder	6	K

Occupation		
Plumber	6	K
Patternmaker	7	M
Printing machine manager	7	M
Telephone engineer	6	I
Site manager, construction	6	K
Capstan setter/operator	7	M
Forest worker	6	J
Auto electrician	6	K
Dental technician	12	O
Watch and clock repairer	6	I
Upholsterer	6	I
Die miller	7	M

PIO

Laboratory technician	8	N
Clerk of Works	6	K
Hatchery manager (fish farm)	6	K
Farm manager	6	J

PSE

Driver/Salesperson, ie, ice cream, ho tdogs, etc.	1	A
Reception engineer (garage)	1	C
Canteen assistant	3	W
Mothers' help	3	W
Room service staff	3	W
Waiter/ress	3	W
Guard, Railways	6	H
Petrol pump attendant	1	C
Riding instructor	12	T
Bus driver	6	L
Undertaker/Embalmer	6	H
Sports assistant	12	T
Patrol (AA/RAC)	6	H
Cleaner	3	W
Dog handler	4	X
Taxi driver	5	G
Cinema projectionist	19	Q
Fence erector	6	K

PSO

Mobile security patrol	4	X
Telephone operator	5	F
Home care assistant, social services	12	U
Hostel assistant	3	W
Nursing auxiliary	12	V
Teacher/craft and design technology	12	U
Coastguard	4	X

PEO

Farm worker	6	J
Hatchery worker	6	J
Tractor driver	6	L
Shelf filler	1	C
Food packer	7	M
Office machinery operator	5	F
Horticultural worker	6	J
Groundsperson	6	J
Demolition worker	6	K
Garment cutter	7	M
Nurseryman/woman	6	J
Sewing machine operator	7	M
Assembly worker	7	M
Moulder/core maker	7	M
Bill poster	6	H
Wood sawyer	7	M
Satellite/TV aerial erector	6	H
Packer	7	H
Crane driver	6	L
Construction plant fitter	6	K
Woodworking machinist	7	M
Sheet metal worker	7	M
Saw doctor	7	M,
Dumper driver	6	L

PAI

Wardrobe assistant/TV dresser	10	Q

Display assistant	10	S
Cake decorator	10	S
Picture framer	6	H
Window dresser	10	S
Musical instrument maker	10	Q
Painter and decorator	6	K
Silversmith	10	S
Floristry assistant	10	S
Chef	3	W
Wig maker	6	H
Dressmaker	6	H
Embroiderer	10	S
Hairdresser	3	W
Sign writer	10	S

PSI

Appliance demonstrator	6	H
Home service adviser	3	W
Ambulance driver	12	V
Hospital porter	12	V
Fireman/woman	4	X
Groom	6	J
Artificial limb fitter	12	V

PEI

Tailor	6	H
Thatcher	6	I
Saddler	6	H
Quality control assistant	7	M
Electronic circuit inspector	7	M
Fault finder (electronics)	7	M
Engineering instructor	7	M
Cowman/woman	6	J
Kennel hand	6	J
Stable hand	6	J
Poultryfarm manager	6	J

POI

Technical assistant (housing - Local Govt)	6	K
Driving examiner	6	H
Game keeper	6	J

PES

Deck officer (Merchant Navy)	6	L
Zoo keeper	6	J
Gas fitter	6	K
Car park attendant	6	H
Jockey	12	T
Domestic appliance servicing	6	I
Roofer	6	K
Lock gate keeper	6	L
Farrier	6	J
Carpenter	6	K
Plasterer	6	K

POS

School caretaker	6	H
Housekeeper	3	W
Kitchen assistant	3	W
Sterile supply worker, hospital	12	O

POE

Engineer/storekeeper	5	G
Golf green keeper	12	T

INVESTIGATIVE OCCUPATIONS

ISP

Chiropodist	12	V
Chiropractor	12	V
Physiotherapist	12	V
Ophthalmic optician	12	O
Orthoptist	12	V

IEO

Osteopath	12	O
Surgeon	12	O
Homeopath	12	V

IEO

Quality control inspector	7	M
Information scientist	8	N
Laundry and dry cleaning manager	2	M
Systems analyst	8	N

IEP

Chemical engineer	7	M
Civil engineer	6	K
Control engineer	7	M
Drilling engineer (oil and gas)	7	M
Electronic engineer	7	M
Energy technologist	7	M
Biomedical engineer	7	M
Brewer	7	M
Rubber technologist	7	M
Structural engineer	6	K
Polymer technologist	7	M
Fuel technologist	7	M
Packing technologist	7	M
Nuclear engineer	7	M
Mechanical engineer	7	M
Food scientist/technologist	7	M
Minerals surveyor	8	N
Mining engineer	7	M
Timber technologist	7	M
Textile technologist	7	M
Geologist	8	N
Forest officer	6	J
Hydrographics surveyor	6	K
Zoologist	6	J

ISA

Museum curator	2	B
Researcher (broadcasting)	10	Q
Town planner	2	B

IES

Dispensing optician	12	V
Environmental engineer	7	M
Retail pharmacist	1	C

ISO

Water engineer	7	M
Environmental health officer	6	H
Factory inspector	6	H
Public analyst	8	N
Dietician	12	V

IPE

Petroleum engineer	7	M
Air traffic engineer	6	L
Fire/burglar alarm engineer	6	I
Instrument mechanic	7	M
Refrigeration and air conditioning mechanic	6	I
Surveyor	6	k

IAS

Conservation officer and restorer	6	K
Landscape architect	10	S

IAP

Broadcasting engineer	7	M
Architect	10	S

IOP

Materials scientist	8	N
Meteorologist	8	N
Metallurgist	8	N
Bacteriologist	8	N

Biochemist	8	N
Biologist	8	N
Botanist	6	J
Geophysicist	8	N
Astronomer	8	N
Physicist	8	N
Chemist	8	N
Archaeologist	8	N
Psychologist	9	P
Patent agent	6	H
Naval architect	7	M

IPA

Dyer	7	M
Industrial photographer	10	S
Reprographic technician	7	M
Colour technologist	7	M
Printing technologist	7	M
Ceramics technologist	7	M
Glass technologist	7	M
Leather technologist	7	M
Lighting engineer	7	M
Paint technologist	7	M

IPO

Patent examiner	7	M
Industrial radiographer	7	M
Air traffic control officer	6	L
Radio officer (Merchant Navy)	6	L
Technical assistant (public health office)	6	H
Dispensing technician, pharmacy	12	O
Biology technician	8	N
Metallurgy technician	7	M
Ergonomist	7	M
Forensic scientist	8	N

IPS

Audiology technician	12	O
Pest control officer	6	H
Neurophysiology technician	12	O
Veterinary surgeon	6	J
Acupuncturist	12	O
Dentist	12	V
Cardiological technician	12	O
Medical laboratory technician	12	O
Medical physics technician	12	O
Radiographer	12	V
Assistant scientific officer/scientific officer (civil service)	8	N
Anaesthetist	12	O

ARTISTIC OCCUPATIONS

ASE

Author	11	R
Drama coach/drama teacher	10	Q
Singer	10	Q
Dancer	11	R

ASI

Music teacher	10	Q
Reviewer/critic	11	R
Art therapist	10	S

AIE

Commercial photographer	10	S
Photo journalist	10	S
Draughts person	10	S
Graphic designer	10	S
Footwear designer	10	S
Kitchen planner	6	H
Visualiser (advertising)	10	S
Film animator	10	Q
Fashion designer	10	S

Costume designer	10	S

AIP

Film cameraman/woman	10	Q
Piano tuner	6	H
Wrought iron smith	6	K
Antique furnisher repairer	6	I
Ceramic painter	10	S
Lighting designer	10	S
Picture restorer	10	S
Wallpaper designer	10	S

AES

Model	6	H
Theatre director	10	Q
TV director	10	Q

AIS

Technical illustrator	10	S
Actor/Actress	10	Q
Composer	10	Q
Editor (Publishing/Newspaper)	11	R
Playwright	11	R

SOCIAL OCCUPATIONS

SEO

Minister of religion	12	U
Education welfare officer	12	U
Social work assistant	12	U
Field social worker	12	U
Careers officer	12	U

SEP

Community centre warden	12	u
Youth and community worker	12	U
Warden, sheltered accommodation	12	U

SEI

Tutor organiser (WEA)	12	U

SEA

Adult literacy organiser	12	U

SPI

Nursery nurse	12	U
Hospital nurse	12	V

SPO

Sheltered workshop supervisor	2	B
Residential social worker	12	U
Day care centre staff, social services	12	U

SIA

Occupational therapist	12	V
Speech therapist	12	V

SIO

Psychiatrist	12	V
Community relations worker	12	U
Medical social worker	12	U
Community development officer	12	U
Psychologist	9	P
Sociologist	9	P

SOE

Visiting officer DHSS	12	U
Road safety officer	12	U
Clerk, social/health services	4	D
Organiser, citizens advice bureau	12	U

Dock police	4	X
Assistant prison governor	4	X
Probation officer	12	U
NSPCC/RSPCC inspector	12	U

SPE

District nurse	12	V
Health visitor	12	V

SIE

Director social services	12	U
Adult education teacher	12	U

SAE

Community drama worker	12	U
Play therapist	12	V
Play leader	12	U

SOP

Organiser of clubs for the disabled	12	U

SAI

Play group organiser	12	U
Nursery school teacher	12	U

ENTERPRISING OCCUPATIONS

EAP

Antique dealer	1	C
Musical instrument sales	1	C
Art director, advertising agency	10	S

EPI

Sales assistant: electrical goods, DIY, car accessories etc.	1	C
Market garden manager	6	J
Car rental sales agent	1	A

ESO

Courier	3	W
Publicity officer	1	A
Human resources manager	2	B
Tour operator	6	H
Cinema/Theatre attendant	12	T
Hotel receptionist	3	W
Betting shop manager	2	B

EIO

Banker	3	E
Commodity broker	1	A
Land agent	2	B
Traffic manager	2	B
Contract manager	2	B
Reader (publishing)	11	R
Transport manager	5	G
Retail manager	1	C
Advertising account executive	1	A
Training officer	2	B
Wholesale distribution manager	5	G
Purchasing officer	2	B
Stock broker's clerk	3	E
Armed forces, commissioned service	4	X

ESI

Market research assistant	1	A
Educational service officer (museum)	12	U
Newsreader (radio, television)	12	T

EOI

Telephone sales person	1	A
Credit club agent	1	A

Private detective	4	X
Marketing executive	1	A
Public relations officer	1	A
Senior editor (publishing)	1	A
Recruiting officer (Ministry of Defence)	1	A
Buyer	1	C

EOS

Classified advertisement sales	1	A
Building society manager	3	E
Sales representative	1	A
Housing manager	2	B
Institutional manager	3	W

EPO

Motor cycle messenger	5	G
Cashier, petrol station	3	E

EIS

Sales negotiator (estate agency)	1	A
Ship and air broker	5	G
Car salesperson	1	A
Auctioneer	1	A
Literary agent	1	A

EAS

Market research interviewer	1	A
Advertising copywriter	11	R
TV writer	11	R
Translator	11	R
Journalist	11	R
Bookseller	1	C

EPS

Supermarket assistant	1	C
Milk roundsman/woman	1	A

ESA

Interpreter	11	R
Box office manager	2	B
Cinema manager	2	B
Theatre manager	10	Q

ESP

Holiday camp staff	3	W
Recreation manager	3	W
Purser	4	X
Public house manager	3	W
Hotel manager	3	W
Institutional manager	3	W

ORGANISATIONAL/ADMINISTRATIVE OCCUPATIONS

OPI

Meter reader	6	H
Audio typist	4	D
Word processor	4	D
Traffic assistant Railways)	6	L
Storekeeper (engineering)	5	G
Filing clerk	4	D

OPS

Medical secretary	4	D
Security guard, airport	4	X

OPE

Farm secretary	4	D

OIS

Research officer, social services	8	N
Solicitor	9	P
Traffic warden	4	X
Library assistant	6	H
Medical records officer	4	D
Customs officer	4	X
Legal executive	9	P
Tax officer	3	X
Local government administrator	2	B
Barristers clerk	9	B
Justices clerk	9	P
Law clerk	9	P

OIE

Actuary	3	E
Tax inspector	3	E
Statistics officer	8	N
Post room clerk	5	G
Accounts clerk	3	E
Building society clerk	3	E
Counter clerk, post office	3	E
Cost accountant	3	E

OSE

Travel agency clerk	4	D
Airline counter clerk	4	D
Pensions information officer	3	E
Pawnbroker	6	H
Health service administrator	2	B
Chief constable	4	X

OSA

Court reporter	11	R
Bilingual secretary	4	D
Conference interpreter	11	R
Arts administrator	10	O

OIP

Ordnance survey surveyor	8	N
Data preparation manager	2	B
Archivist	6	H

OSP

Home care organiser	12	U
Nursing officer	12	V

OEP

Stock controller	5	G
Proof reader	11	R

OSI

Clerical officer/assistant, civil service	4	D
Ward clerk	4	D
Optician's receptionist	6	H
Rent officer	3	E
Court officer	9	P
Usher to magistrates' court	9	P
Funeral director	6	H

OEI

Shipping clerk	5	G
Import/export clerk	5	G
Claims officer (insurance)	3	E
Company secretary	2	B
Accounting technician	3	E
Insurance underwriter	3	E

OES

Chartered clerk (air bookings)	5	G
Sales ledger clerk	3	E
Car hire manager	2	B

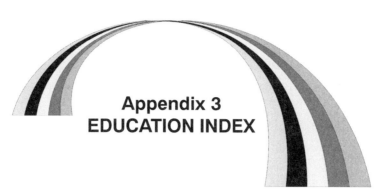

Appendix 3
EDUCATION INDEX

This appendix lists education courses which might correspond to your skills and interests as explored in the section WHO AM I? It is subdivided into four sections: Data, Things, People and Ideas.

DATA

Business
Accounting
Banking and Finance
Business Management and Administration
Healthcare Administration
Hotel Management
Insurance
Marketing and Sales
Medical Records Administration
Real Estate/Property Management
Secretarial Studies and office Administration

Computer and Information Sciences
Computer and information Sciences
Data Processing

Law
Law

Library and Archival Sciences
Library Science

Mathematics
Mathematics

Physical and Life Sciences
Astronomy
Atmospheric Science
Chemistry
General Physical Science
Geology
Life Sciences
Oceanography
Physics
Science Technologies

Public Affairs and Protective Services
Criminal Justice
Fire Control
Public Administration
Recreation
Social Service

THINGS

Agriculture and Natural Resources
Agricultural Business and Management
Agricultural Production and Services
Animal Science
Fisheries and Wildlife Sciences
Food Science and Technology
Forest Technology and Products
Forestry and natural Resources
Horticulture and Landscaping
Marine Technology
Soil and Plant Sciences

Consumer and Personal Services
Animal Grooming and Training
Custodial Services
Floral Design
Funeral Service
Hair Design
Personal Services
Upholstering and Leatherworking

Engineering
Engineering
Engineering Technologies

Equipment and Construction
Auto Body Repair
Aviation Maintenance
Aviation Management
Construction Trades
Drafting
Electricity and Electronics Repair
Flight Training
Gas and Diesel Mechanics
Heating and Cooling Mechanics
Industrial Mechanics
Instrument Repair
Metalworking
Precision Production Work
Small Engine Repair
Vehicle and Equipment Operation
Woodworking

PEOPLE

Business
Accounting
Banking and Finance
Business Management and Administration
Healthcare Administration
Hotel Management
Insurance
Marketing and Sales
Medical Records Administration
Real Estate/Property Management
Secretarial Studies and office Administration

Consumer and Personal Services
Animal Grooming and Training
Custodial Services
Floral Design
Funeral Service
Hair Design
Personal Services
Upholstering and Leatherworking

Education
Counselling
Early Childhood and Elementary Education
Education Administration
Health and Physical Administration
Secondary Education
Special Education

Health
Allied Dental Services
Allied Veterinary Services
Chiropractic
Dentistry
Emergency Medical Care
Medical Assisting
Medical Laboratory Techniques
Medicine
Naturopathic Medicine
Nursing
Optical Services
Optometry
Other Health Technologies
Pharmacy
Public Health
Radiologic Technology
Rehabilitation Services
Respiratory Therapy
Speech Pathology and Audiology
Veterinary Medicine

Home Economics
Child Development and Child Care
Clothing and Textiles
Dietetics
Food Service
Home Economics

Law
Law

Psychology
Psychology

Public Affairs and Protecive Services
Criminal Justice
Fire Control
Public Administration
Recreation
Social Service

Social Sciences
Anthropology
Area and Ethnic Studies
Economics
General Social Science
Geography
History
Political Science
Sociology

Theology, Religion and Philosophy
Philosophy
Religion
Theology

IDEAS

Architecture and Environmental Design
Architecture and Environmental Design

Communication Technologies
Communication Technologies
Journalism and Communications

Computer and information Sciences
Computer and information Sciences
Data Processing

Fine Arts
Art
Dance
Dramatic Arts
Modelling
Music
Photographic Arts
Printing and Graphics

Letters
English Literature
Foreign Languages
Liberal Studies
Speech

Mathematics
Mathematics

Physical and Life Sciences
Astronomy
Atmospheric Science
Chemistry
General Physical Science
Geology
Life Sciences
Oceanography
Physics
Science Technologies

Social Sciences
Anthropology
Area and Ethnic Studies
Economics
General Social Science
Geography
History
Political Science
Sociology

Theology, Religion and Philosophy
Philosophy
Religion
Theology

Appendix 4
LEISURE ACTIVITIES

There follow six lists of leisure activities that correspond with your interests as measured by the questionnaire on page 63. The lists suggest activities that might be of interest to you. This does not imply that you will have the necessary skills, only the motivation.

PRACTICAL
repairing or mending things
bike or horse riding
walking/hiking
camping
playing football, cricket, hockey, netball
making things like model aircraft, dresses, etc, using patterns
 or instruction kits
cooking
gardening
do-it-yourself
mountain climbing
ice-skating
roller-skating
aerobic dancing
skiing
skin diving/scuba diving
bicycling alone for exercise
working out in a gym
jogging alone
swimming
archery
training animals
hang-gliding,
sky diving
carpentry
candle-making
wine-making
sewing

INVESTIGATIVE
developing and processing photos
reading books and magazines on scientific or technical
 subjects
observing, collecting. identifying such things as birds,
 animals, plants, fossils, shells, rocks etc.
visiting museums, scientific or technical displays
watching and listening to documentaries or "in-depth" reports
 on TV and radio
playing chess, draughts, bridge, scrabble, mastermind, or
 other games of skill
computer programming
genealogy
self-development
meditation
attending lectures

SOCIAL
visiting and working with the handicapped, old people, etc.
taking part in guides, scouts, youth groups, etc.
planning and giving parties

attending sports events, pop concerts, films etc, with a group
 of friends
helping to raise funds for a charity
working with young children in play groups, sunday schools,
 cubs, brownies etc.
activities with the family
massage
spending social time with friends, at pubs, dinner parties,
 restaurants
joining clubs or activities primarily for the social functions eg,.
 church, choral group, political party, drama club
sailing with others

ARTISTIC
playing a musical instrument or singing
writing short stories or poetry
sketching, drawing or painting
taking part in plays or musicals
craft work, eg, pottery, weaving, knitting, jewellery makiny.
 macrame, etc
visiting art galleries, exhibitions, plays or concerts
flower arranging
yoga
photography
gem polishing
interior decorating
restoring antiques
sculpting

ENTERPRISING
playing monopoly, backgammon, poker or other games of chance
doing small jobs, such as gardening or car repair work for a fee
taking part in debates or making speeches
following politics in the newspaper or on radio or TV
being on a committee
earning money by selling things
games where winning is important - squash, tennis,
 badminton, soccer, rugby, snooker, darts, cards, bicycle and
 motor racing (if winning is not important - the interest will be
 more social)
winemaking to save money
entering craft work in competitions

ORGANISATIONAL/ADMINISTRATIVE
using typewriters, calculators, computers for record keeping
keeping detailed accounts or a careful diary
tidying up sheds, cupboards, drawers, etc.
keeping times and recording results at sporting events
collecting and cataloguing coins, stamps, photo albums,
 scrap books
calligraphy